BY COMPTON MACKENZIE

Novels and Romances

SINISTER STREET
SYLVIA SCARLETT
GUY AND PAULINE
CARNIVAL
FIGURE OF EIGHT
CORAL
THE VANITY GIRL
ROGUES AND VAGABONDS
THE ALTAR STEPS
THE PARSON'S PROGRESS
THE HEAVENLY LADDER
HUNTING THE FAIRIES
WHISKY GALORE
KEEP THE HOME GUARD TURNING
THE MONARCH OF THE GLEN
THE RIVAL MONSTER
BEN NEVIS GOES EAST
THE RED TAPEWORM
PAPER LIVES
ROCKETS GALORE
THE STOLEN SOPRANO
THE LUNATIC REPUBLIC
POOR RELATIONS
APRIL FOOLS
RICH RELATIVES
BUTTERCUPS AND DAISIES
WATER ON THE BRAIN
VESTAL FIRE
EXTRAORDINARY WOMEN
THIN ICE
EXTREMES MEET
THE THREE COURIERS
OUR STREET
THE DARKENING GREEN
THE PASSIONATE ELOPEMENT
FAIRY GOLD
THE SEVEN AGES OF WOMAN
PARADISE FOR SALE
MEZZOTINT
THE FOUR WINDS OF LOVE:
    THE EAST WIND
    THE SOUTH WIND
    THE WEST WIND
    THE NORTH WIND

Play

THE LOST CAUSE

Verse

POEMS 1907
KENSINGTON RHYMES

History and Biography

EASTERN EPIC. VOL. I
ALL OVER THE PLACE
GALLIPOLI MEMORIES

ATHENIAN MEMORIES
GREEK MEMORIES
AEGEAN MEMORIES
WIND OF FREEDOM
MR ROOSEVELT
DR BENES
PRINCE CHARLIE
PRINCE CHARLIE AND HIS LADIES
CATHOLICISM AND SCOTLAND
MARATHON AND SALAMIS
PERICLES
THE WINDSOR TAPESTRY
THE VITAL FLAME
I TOOK A JOURNEY
COALPORT
REALMS OF SILVER
THE QUEEN'S HOUSE
MY RECORD OF MUSIC
SUBLIME TOBACCO
GREECE IN MY LIFE
CATS' COMPANY
CATMINT
LOOK-AT CATS

Essays and Criticism

ECHOES
A MUSICAL CHAIR
UNCONSIDERED TRIFLES
REAPED AND BOUND
LITERATURE IN MY TIME
ON MORAL COURAGE

Children's Stories

LITTLE CAT LOST
SANTA CLAUS IN SUMMER
TOLD
MABEL IN QUEER STREET
THE UNPLEASANT VISITORS
THE CONCEITED DOLL
THE ENCHANTED BLANKET
THE DINING-ROOM BATTLE
THE ADVENTURES OF TWO CHAIRS
THE ENCHANTED ISLAND
THE NAUGHTYMOBILE
THE FAIRY IN THE WINDOW BOX
THE STAIRS THAT KEPT ON GOING
    DOWN
THE STRONGEST MAN ON EARTH
THE SECRET ISLAND
BUTTERFLY HILL

Autobiography

MY LIFE AND TIMES: OCTAVE ONE;
OCTAVE TWO; OCTAVE THREE;
OCTAVE FOUR; OCTAVE FIVE;
OCTAVE SIX; OCTAVE SEVEN;
OCTAVE EIGHT; OCTAVE NINE

The author working on Octave One of *My Life and Times*

MY LIFE AND TIMES

OCTAVE TEN

1953-1963

Compton Mackenzie

1971
CHATTO & WINDUS
LONDON

Published by
Chatto & Windus Ltd
42 William IV Street
London, W.C.2

★

Clarke, Irwin & Co. Ltd
Toronto

ISBN 0 7011 1703 6

Printed in Great Britain by
T. & A. Constable Ltd
Hopetoun Street, Edinburgh

To

IAN CHATTO and NORAH WINDUS

gratefully and affectionately

or in other words

IAN PARSONS and NORAH SMALLWOOD

with a thought for

HAROLD RAYMOND

CONTENTS

*

ACKNOWLEDGMENTS

My grateful thanks for permission to quote letters are due to the following: Mrs Joy Adamson, Sir Gerald Beadle, Mr Edmund Blunden, Mr Ian Gilmour, Mgr. Neil Mackellaig, Mrs Diana Menuhin, Admiral of the Fleet Earl Mountbatten of Burma, Mr Nigel Nicolson, Mr Eric Roberts, Mgr. Hugh Somers, Mrs Tamara Talbot Rice, The Rt. Hon. Lord Thomson of Fleet, Mr Rex Warner, Mr Herbert Wilcox; and to Mr Winston Churchill for the late Mr Randolph Churchill, Mrs Veronica Gosling for the late Mr Robert Henriques, Mrs Thelma Holland for the late Mr Vyvyan Holland, Mrs Thelma Cazalet-Keir for the late Mr David Keir, Mgr. Neil Mackellaig for the late Mgr. Dominic Mackellaig, the Literary Executor of W. Somerset Maugham, Mr Nigel Nicolson for the late Sir Harold Nicolson, Mrs Berta Onions for the late Mr Oliver Onions, Mr Anthony Sells for the late Vice-Admiral W. F. Sells, Miss Catherine Simpson for the late Mr T. B. Simpson, Mrs Helen Thurber for the late Mr James Thurber, Lady Sarita Vansittart for the late Robert Gilbert Vansittart, 1st Baron of Denham.

I would like to offer my apologies to those literary heirs whom I have been unable to trace. I hope they will accept this general acknowledgment for material I have quoted.

C.M.

LIST OF ILLUSTRATIONS

STILL SEVENTY YEARS OLD: 1953

I SET out on September 2nd, 1969, the birthday of my wife Lily, to write the last volume of *My Life and Times*. Exactly a year before on that date David Keir[1] had written:

"Let me know when you are likely to be in London on your way back to Edinburgh so that we can have our usual party. . . . We think much of you both and are looking forward to your forthcoming spate of works. Thelma sends you both much love, as I do always too.
Affectionately,
David."

In June of this year when we passed through Paris on our way back to Pradelles we were shocked to read in *The Times* of David Keir's death. In two successive summers I had lost two of my dearest friends, both about twenty years younger than myself.

At the end of my last Octave I wrote about the heartwarming dinner which, under David's management, was given to me by my fellow-members of the Savile. What I forgot to say was that Thelma had supplied the flowers from that wonderful flower-shop she used to run in Sloane Street.

I find a letter from David Keir written to me on February 5th, 1953:

All my loyalties are strangely divided at present between Edinburgh, Glasgow, Paisley and Glenfinnan. Your letter chased me about for some days. It was kind of you to write about the Savile dinner but that's the very least I would do. Certainly no one seemed out of humour that night and with equal certainty they were all delighted to honour you. But then the whole of those few days at Raspit[2] and the Savile were fun and John Moore is always a good companion on such occasions.

I go back to Edinburgh tomorrow for excavations in the Register House and then face the prospect of some days in the Paisley Public Library next week. What things we do!

Much love, dear Monty. I may even be in Edinburgh when you arrive about the 19th. If I am no doubt we shall together look through a glass brightly, if not in the Savile soon.

[1] The late David Keir, M.B.E.
[2] The Keirs' country house near Sevenoaks.

David Keir's sojourn in Paisley must have been for the research he was doing for his history of the cotton and thread kings, Coates and Clark. He wrote several histories of great businesses besides editing the last Statistical Account of Edinburgh. One of these, the history of adventure across the Atlantic in *The Bowring Story*, he generously dedicated to me in these words:

"To the youngest of my oldest friends."

When he left us in this June of 1969 he had all but finished the history of W. H. Smith and Son which will be another monument to the enthusiasm, industry, painstaking accuracy and elegant lucidity of his style. I find it hard to believe that during next winter I shall not hear his jolly voice at the other end of the telephone to say that he will be round at Drummond Place soon after.

I recall so many hours, small hours often, when I have enjoyed the best of talk with him and that other 'good companion' John Moore, but my personal grief must not allow me to forget the value of the work that survives them—John Moore's work for the English countryside and David Keir's work for Scotland.

It is sad that David died before he had the joy of hearing that his dear friend Malcolm MacDonald[1] had been awarded the O.M. It was Malcolm MacDonald who would give the moving and eloquent address on the occasion of the memorial service for David Keir at St Columba's Church of Scotland on June 25th, 1969. That address finished with these words:

"In a book of poems which he composed and published more than forty years ago—when he was in his earliest twenties—he wrote these words in a piece called 'An Epitaph'.

> This is quietness—a still long sleep
> In a world of slumber, kind and deep.
> . . . the mind to rest is lain
> And there is no more stirring, no more pain.

We miss him greatly and pay loving homage to his memory."

But I must go back to 1953 when David Keir was one of those who convinced me that in making what I believed would be my final home in Edinburgh I had decided wisely.

Chrissie was right in thinking that 31 Drummond Place was the best of the many possible abodes we had looked at. Drummond

[1] Rt. Hon. Malcolm John MacDonald, O.M., P.C., son of Ramsay MacDonald.

Place was the first addition made to the New Town after Waterloo. The building of it began in October 1815 and in consequence all the floors in Drummond Place are of soft wood. The oak that went to building our ships was not available for domestic use until Moray Place was built some twenty years later.

31 and 32 Drummond Place had been bought by a Sheriff Substitute called Carrick Allen, who had made a perfect entrance-floor flat by adding to 31 the two rooms on the left of the entrance hall of 32. He had left 32 with its own basement, but he had knocked together the sub-basements of 31 and 32 so that we had two gardens on a level with our sub-basement at the back. In the houses farther along, the rising slope put them below surface level behind, as they all were in front.

At this date it was touch and go whether Drummond Place would maintain the dignity it had enjoyed until the Second War had over 'popularised' it. The railings of the big central garden had been pulled down in that fatuous campaign for scrap iron, and the residents were just getting together to re-fence the garden and prevent it becoming the playground of destructive youngsters.

I realised we should have to spend a good deal on redecoration, putting up shelves for my library and rewiring the electricity. When the electricity people were at work I told them to get rid of a single bulb in the room which was to be my workroom.

"Would you mind if we took this bulb away with us for our museum?"

"For your museum? Why?"

"Well, sir, we reckon this bulb has been going since 1878 when Edinburgh houses started getting electricity."

"Do you mean to tell me that bulb is five years older than I am?"

If any of our bulbs lasted for three months today we should brag about them.

When the expense of getting 31 Drummond Place into order was beginning to seem a little difficult, luckily Faith's cottage in Majorca was sold, and although it took several months before the Bank of England was able to allow one British subject to buy a property from another British subject in a foreign land, the sale was finally permitted.

Betty and Ursula Maxwell had started a firm of antiques and interior decoration during the war, and to Galloways went the job of transforming 31 Drummond Place, to which we hoped to move from Denchworth Manor in September.

Faith left Majorca in April and went to recover from the rigours of a Majorca winter in Nice. I had decided to risk taking on a lease of the flat in Sheffield Terrace discovered by Chrissie and Rosemary Russell before Faith was able to see it herself. To my great relief when she arrived back in May she was delighted with it. 13c Sheffield Terrace looked out over one of those Campden Hill Gardens. I hope some of those gardens of once upon a time are not yet covered by those dreary ant-heaps of reinforced concrete.

I did a great deal of broadcasting throughout this year, and also a fair amount of televising. I think it is true to say that television made its first real impact on what were called viewers with its successful pictures of the Coronation. Besides Richard Dimbleby's masterly commentary the cameras showed a triumphant advance on anything that the public had yet watched.

From broadcasts I recall with pleasure one called *Beaux and Belles*, which was produced, I think, by the Overseas Service whose headquarters were in Oxford Street. I was impressed by what I thought the more agreeable atmosphere of Oxford Street than at Broadcasting House where there was a lot of petty jealousy of Overseas. I recall a discussion quartet between Lord Russell, Aneurin Bevan, Lord Byers and myself, which was so well received in the East that Overseas asked Broadcasting House if they would like to do a repeat for home consumption. In spite of the fact that they would have had to pay the four speakers only half of their fifteen guinea fee Broadcasting House did not think people at home would be interested.

In *Beaux and Belles* I had to interview four stage stars of the past against a background of the music with which their names were associated. The late Hubert Clifford, an Australian composer and brilliant conductor, was in charge of the performances at what was once upon a time the Avenue Theatre at the end of Northumberland Avenue which the B.B.C. had taken over, after it became the Playhouse.

My first star of the past was Lady Hicks, who as Ellaline Terriss sang *Just a Little Bit of String* in *The Shop Girl*, which I had been whistling in my teens. At this date Lady Hicks was 82. If I am a year out I beg the pardon of that enchanting old lady who is now 98.

My next star of the past was Ada Reeve. She wrote an interesting volume of memories for which she did me the honour of asking for a foreword. As I remember, Ada Reeve was 80 when her book was published. Phyllis Monkman was next, with memories of the Co-optimists. The last was Muriel George, and I was back with the

Follies listening to *Moon, Moon, Serenely Shining.* Muriel George was the mother of John Davenport. Nobody I have ever known messed up his life so successfully as John Davenport. He had a first-class brain but instead of getting down to the books he was going to write he wrote reviews for the *Observer.* The unwritten book I regret most was the life of Norman Douglas he was proposing to write. He was a brilliant pianist but never could discipline himself to the hard work that the life of a professional musician requires. He was one of the two strongest men I have known and his feats of strength, when displayed as they sometimes were in a temper, were constantly getting him into trouble; one of these caused his resignation from the Savile. Some of us tried hard to get him re-elected but the election committee always refused. They were not prepared to risk the chance of another Savilian being picked up by John Davenport, taken outside into Brook Street and dropped in the gutter.

The television programme I enjoyed most was a talk about cats in which I had about half a dozen cats on my lap one after another. Cats are not fond of behaving as you want them to behave at any given moment, and I warned the producer that it might be a *mauvais quart d'heure* for television. However, every cat behaved kindly, and I had a number of letters, some of which I hope to reproduce one day when I make my collection of *Whiskers Galore* from the letters I have received from all over the world about cats. I had a delicious wee Abyssinian kitten in my arms to talk about but I was unable to get hold of a Manx cat. However, I did talk a bit about the character of Manx cats with admiration and was gratified to receive a letter from the Isle of Man Tourist Board:

"Just a line to say how much pleasure your recent reference to the Manx cat gave people over here.

"You may not be aware that recently a Society for the Protection of the Manx Cat was formed in the Isle of Man, where the numbers of Manx Cats are showing a serious decline due to mixed breeding and the export of pure Manx Cats to the United Kingdom and America."

I wrote about my beloved Twinkle in my Third Octave. I should like to be reassured by some kind reader of this Octave whether that Society still exists and whether their work on behalf of the Manx Cat has been successful.

One other television show in which I took part at Bristol may provide a smile. This was a try-out of the very popular *Any Questions* of broadcasting as a TV attraction.

It was always a particular pleasure to broadcast from Bristol where Gerald Beadle,[1] the Controller of West Regional, and Frank Gillard had done such splendid service during and after the war. My nephew Nicholas Crocker had been chosen to be trained for television and he was directing the cameras for that *Any Questions*, part of his job being to direct the studio audience. I managed to disgrace the family by knocking over a jug of water with one of my too emphatic gestures when answering a question about Lord Nuffield. I was recalling the way he had impressed me as an undergraduate when he told me that Morris's Oxford Garage he had just opened would not hold the cars in ten years' time and how I had written an article to warn the University that they must make a road round it passing through Christ Church Meadows. In the middle of Christ Church Meadows I upset the glass.

When *Any Questions* was over I found that the Press were ringing up Bristol to ask what the B.B.C. were going to do about my having used a 'naughty word'.

"Naughty word?" I enquired.

"Yes, when you upset the water they thought you exclaimed 'Christ!'; they missed Christ Church. There are some reporters anxious to talk to you."

So I realised what had happened and I remember saying to them:

"Why I can be perfectly sure that I could not have exclaimed 'Christ' is because in my young days we thought that any fellow who exclaimed 'Christ' was a bounder. We weren't shocked by the profanity, we were shocked by his manners. I have never used 'Christ' anywhere in my novels as an exclamation."

I was deeply touched to find that Horace Vachell had driven all the way from Sherborne to see me.

I find a letter from 'Mac',[2] that beloved blind professor of Imperial History of whom I have written in Octave 9:

> "University of Bristol,
> Department of History
> 24th March 1953

Dear Monty,

I should like to say how much we all enjoyed your visit last night. There is no doubt it gave Horace Vachell a great deal of pleasure.

---

[1] Sir Gerald Beadle, C.B.E.
[2] Emeritus Professor C. M. MacInnes.

He had come up from Sherborne for the sole reason of meeting you, which I think is a very good effort for a man of ninety-two. All of us here are devoted to him, and we fear that we are not likely to enjoy his company very much longer. That added additional value to your visit since it gave our dear old friend pleasure. . . .

Yours ever
Mac"

When he waved goodbye to me from his car on his way back to Sherborne late that night it was my farewell to Horace Annesley Vachell who was a Lieutenant in the Rifle Brigade in the year I was born. Soon after that he gave up the army and went out to California of which he has written delightful memories. But I suppose *The Hill*, a novel about his old school Harrow, was the best known of the many books he wrote. His vitality was magnificent. His last sheaf of memoirs was published when he was 90, and he was writing away when in July 1955 death came to him kindly. He was seated at his desk, a glass of port beside him, and writing an article. Suddenly he leant over and without a sound passed away, the glass of port half-drunk, the article half-written. Was any other writer granted so enviable a death?

When I got back to Denchworth from Bristol I found a letter from George Bruce in Aberdeen:

"I understand from the President of the Aberdeen University Debater that you are to take part with Mr Gilbert Harding in a discussion on the afternoon of 22nd April. The B.B.C. would like to record the debate with a view to a possible broadcast."

This was the second year of Jimmy Edwards' term of office as Rector. His election, although he was himself the son of a professor, was such a shock to academic opinion that the Senate did not give him the usual Honorary LL.D. to add to his D.F.C. This debate was being financed by Jimmy Edwards, and those taking part in it were to be student representatives of every university in Great Britain and Ireland. I regretfully confess that I have forgotten what the motion was, proposed by Gilbert Harding and opposed by me, but I remember I won by a very narrow majority.

It had been arranged that Gilbert and I were to go up to Aberdeen by the 7.30 p.m. train from King's Cross. Gilbert had been drinking rather much lately and I told him that if he did not present himself at King's Cross in a state of icy sobriety I should refuse to go north with him. Chrissie and I found him at King's Cross in a state of

B

melancholic sobriety. We were sitting in the lighted dining-car in the April dusk when Gilbert wanted to look at the tower of—was it a church in Grantham? He called to a dining-car steward and asked him to turn off the light. This the steward did to the obvious discomfort of the diners. Certainly the tower looked much better in the April dusk without electric light but the diners thought their plates looked better with the lights on.

When we reached Aberdeen next morning we were met by the President of the Debater who told us they thought we should be more comfortable at a private hotel than at the Station Hotel, and we were driven to a cosy little hotel in one of Aberdeen's many attractive streets. We were to be called for at eleven to be shown the various features of Aberdeen, including the fish market.

"I must have a whisky," Gilbert said to me when we were seated in the comfortable sitting-room. "If we're going to be dragged round a fish market I must have a whisky."

"Unfortunately, my dear Gilbert, it's a temperance hotel, and you can't have even one whisky."

I see now the look of despair on poor Gilbert Harding's face.

Chrissie must have been so moved by that expression that she went off to consult the landlady. Some minutes later that kindly woman came in with a bottle of Younger's ale and a glass.

"With the compliments of the house," she said as she put them down on the small table beside Gilbert's chair.

As we drove round Aberdeen with our students' escort I was back in Aberdeen 47 years earlier in a cloudless February, rehearsing my first play which would be produced in Edinburgh in the following week. I have been lucky always to find the sun shining in Aberdeen, and its granite glittering.

We were due to lunch at the Union before the debate. Just as we were going in Gilbert caught sight, on the left, of a sign indicating a bar now open. He made a dive for it but I gripped him hard.

"No, no, Gilbert. Not until the debate is over."

We sat on wooden benches for lunch, the principal dish of which was venison.

"I can't bear venison," Gilbert groaned. "And venison moreover with nothing but water to drink."

In spite of, or perhaps because of, having had nothing to drink but water Gilbert made an excellent speech. The only one of the students representing his university who made an outstanding speech was the young man who came from Trinity College, Dublin.

After the debate was over we were invited to refresh ourselves at the Station Hotel where Gilbert Harding drank enough whisky to recover from what for him had been a day of drought.

It was Charities Week for the Aberdeen students and after attending a performance of the revue at Her Majesty's Theatre we were due to attend the ball with which Charities Week concluded. My job was to crown the Charities Queen at the end of it.

When we reached Her Majesty's Theatre the manager took me aside to say that *Whisky Galore* had been there the previous week to record business.

"Will I give you a wee souvenir?" he murmured.

The souvenir was a bottle of whisky which I slipped into the pocket of my greatcoat.

Gilbert, Chrissie and I were given seats in the third row of the dress circle; in front of Gilbert was a lady of abundant *décolletage*. The revue had not been going for ten minutes when Gilbert began to doze. I noticed his head drooping slowly lower and lower until his moustache reached the back of the neck of the lady in front of him. Then he threw up his head with a gasp. After trying to keep awake for a while he would begin to nod again and once more be woken up with a start by finding his moustache against a female neck. At the end of the act the *decollétée* lady retired from her seat, which remained empty during the second act. Now Gilbert Harding was woken up by the back of a stall instead of the back of a lady's neck.

It was about two o'clock when Gilbert, Chrissie and I got back to our hotel. Chrissie went off to bed; she and I were going to Edinburgh next day. Gilbert had to leave for London at some very early hour; in spite of that he sat up talking until at last I said:

"I know you are getting up so early, dear Gilbert, that it's hardly worth your while to go to bed, but my train to Edinburgh will let me have a few hours' sleep and I am going to bed."

As we reached the passage and bade each other a somewhat paradoxical goodnight, Gilbert asked suddenly:

"Did I see the manager at the theatre give you something?"

"Yes, he gave me a bottle of whisky. All right, Gilbert, I know what a day you've had."

I went back into the sitting-room and took the bottle from my coat. "You'd better have it," I told him.

I still see that much-loved friend on his way to a brief rest with that bottle of whisky clasped to his heart.

"You look like an old maid going off to bed with her hot water bottle, Gilbert."

"Don't talk to me about water," said Gilbert, shuddering at the memory of the water at lunch.

To my regret I never met Lord Vansittart[1] but we exchanged one or two letters. I still find it hard to understand how our politicians failed to heed the warnings he gave them about Germany during the 'thirties. On March 12th, he wrote to me from Denham Place:

"Dear Sir Compton,

You wrote to me some time ago in connection with a broadcast that I had made on behalf of the Poles. May I now consult you on another matter which, as I know from your published letters, also concerns you.

"I have long ago thought that the present method of taxing writers and artists is highly unjust and reprehensible, and though I hardly ever speak in the House except on international affairs I had for some time thought of taking up the cudgels on their behalf and carrying the matter to a division—the only way of getting it considered seriously. I consulted Sir Alan Herbert on the project, but I doubted whether I was the right person for the part and also got no encouragement from him, so I abandoned the idea. I still think that somebody else would be better qualified, and I might try to find him. But if I do so, would you, or any other of your friends, be willing to provide me with a concise brief of grievances? I know all the broad lines of course but I am not—for instance—quite sure of what happened in the case of your own copyrights, to which I have seen reference in the Press.

Yours sincerely,
Vansittart"

I wrote a long letter to Lord Vansittart in which I told him of the talks Alan Herbert and I had had with the Chancellor of the Exchequer and Somerset House in which we had pleaded for a spread of authors' earnings for the demands of Income Tax. They had once been allowed over three years. I went on:

"The abolition of the spread of Income Tax is worrying us greatly. For instance next year or the year after I shall almost certainly have to have an eye operation which may prevent my writing

[1] Robert Gilbert Vansittart, P.C., G.C.B., G.C.M.G., M.V.O., 1st Baron of Denham.

anything for a year, but by the present regulation I am debarred from making enough income now to pay for what may be a year of idleness. Problems like mine are now confronting all authors, young and old, successful and unsuccessful.''

Vansittart wrote back:

''. . . in view of what you tell me I think I must in any case hold my hand for the present, seeing that you and Alan Herbert have had a long personal talk with Rab Butler and also that you have headed a deputation to Somerset House. If I put down any motion *now* it seems clear that I should only get the old official hand-off that authoritative discussions have taken place and 'the matter is under consideration'. There is nothing anyhow to be done in regard to *this* Budget. If, however, you and Alan Herbert find that nothing concrete has come out of your discussions with Rab, then I might consider trying to get a debate in the late summer or at the beginning of the autumn. Meanwhile, I suppose the right tactics would be for you two to prod the Chancellor at intervals . . . and to carry out the same tactics at Somerset House. If the prodding produces nothing but an impression of inertia perhaps you would let me know. A debate would be all the more effective if all other remedies had been exhausted—and patience too.''

Fortunately Rab Butler had a genuine desire to help literature and gave authors a two years' spread; no doubt he would have retrieved the three years' spread if Somerset House and the Treasury had let him.

I was very glad to get a letter from Bernard Fergusson[1] that March about the Queen Mary broadcast which had been a nerve-racking hour talking to various people all over Great Britain, praying that the telephone would behave itself. He wrote from Versailles:

My dear Monty,

My wife and I have just finished listening to your programme on Queen Mary. It was most moving; it couldn't have been bettered, and your Aberdeenshire dominie nearly made me 'greet'.

May heaven bless and most grateful congratulations.

The congratulations should really have been sent to Christopher Sykes and Douglas Cleverdon who had the job of constructing that broadcast; I only did the talking. When we started the programme Queen Mary became very ill and the B.B.C. decided we must do the programme twice, once as an obituary in case she died. I was

[1] Brigadier Sir Bernard Fergusson, G.C.M.G.

anxious to tell the story I told about her as a girl which I related in
Octave Four but not knowing whether a story of her girlhood would
be well received now I asked her great friend Lady Airlie to find out
for me. A message came from Marlborough House to say there would
be no objection to my telling the story if it was true, as no doubt it was.

The B.B.C. heads were much bucked when Queen Mary graciously
let them know that she herself had much enjoyed the broadcast.

In that March I received an encouraging letter from Mr Melville
Proctor in the Department of English at the University of
California:

"I have been working for some two years now on a large group
of novels about Oxford and Cambridge, with results which I hope
will be published soon by the University of California Press. My
investigations began with nineteenth century novels (more than a
hundred in all), but inevitably they have led me on to more recent
works, of which the second part of *Sinister Street* is by far the most
distinguished. Viewing it against the background of its predecessors
it seems to me to have created for the first time—and more effectively
than any of its successors—a heightened and sustained concept of
what Oxford could mean to the individual. It has been my special
task to trace this concept . . . but nowhere is it stated as effectively
as in your novel."

The letter went on to wonder why there were so few novels about
Cambridge and whether the later novels about Oxford had been
influenced by Newman's *The Idea of a University*.

"I hope that I am not imposing upon you by asking if you yourself have felt this association with Newman's. . . ."

In view of the fact that in this year 1969 *Sinister Street* has been
again reprinted by Macdonalds and Penguin and that the B.B.C.
did a version of it in six episodes, I think it is worth reprinting what
I wrote to Mr Proctor in 1953. I should be telling him if I wrote to
him today that more and more women were writing to me about
Sinister Street.

"You are certainly right in attributing to myself a belief that
the value of a university for an undergraduate is what you call
'association with minds as young and enquiring as his own', but I
hesitate to admit any influence, at any rate on, myself of Newman's
Idea of a University. In my case Matthew Arnold was the only
slight influence.

"I think the reason why Cambridge has produced so few novels has been its greater devotion to academic education. Nevertheless, today I find more of the Oxford of my youth in King's College, Cambridge than in any Oxford College. At the same time, a desire among Oxford undergraduates for the old University life is apparent, and it is of some significance that the republication of *Sinister Street* after going out of print during the war years has had what I hope, without arrogance, I may call a civilising effect.

"*Sinister Street* suffered from the numerous progeny it engendered, but most of them have long been forgotten, and *Sinister Street* is now too remote to seem merely dated.

"May I venture to point out that in my opinion one of the reasons why university life lives in *Sinister Street* is that I deliberately confined my undergraduates to their ages. Therefore the absurdities, the snobberies, the enthusiasms and the prejudices are those of young men without experience of the world. I was 30 myself when I wrote the book but I never allowed my principal character to be more than 22. I look forward with interest to your book because I realise that you have penetrated into the heart of the matter."

The reason why I took on so much work of various kinds this year was the expectation that I would probably have to have an operation on my eyes and that this might lead to as much as a year of doing no work with them. With that money to find after losing my appeal against the Income Tax claim, I had to accept a generous offer for a book about Buckingham Palace which I called *The Queen's House* and also for some very well paid articles about Windsor Castle. I was worried by my inability to carry on with the second volume of *Eastern Epic* but this would take at the very least six months of hard work with masses of sometimes almost illegible military reports.

It must have been my disappointment at not being able to get on with *Eastern Epic* that made me choose *Ben Nevis Goes East* for my next novel. However, when I had written only a couple of chapters, Edward Liveing came along to ask if I would tackle the job of writing a history of the Chartered Bank of India, Australia and China to mark their century. The fee was to be a generous one. I started to write it in August and in spite of having the move to Edinburgh in the middle of it, I managed to finish it in October. The book was called *Realms of Silver* and I was fascinated by the adventures of silver during the nineteenth century. I had never realised quite what an ill effect the cheapening of silver by the West was going to have on the East.

My old age has been enriched by many Edinburgh friendships, though too often impoverished by the loss of old friends. One of those who left us in this year 1969 was Jack Lennie. I see him now with the mind's eye after he had driven me back from the Arts Club to Drummond Place while we were still in the confusion of the move from Berkshire.

"Now, don't forget to ring me at once if there is anything I can do to help."

In 1953 Jack Lennie was still running the family business of opticians; that renowned business has now been incorporated. He had married a most lovable and intelligent Italian and they had two delightful children, Paul and Nadina. They left Edinburgh a few years after we came to live there but returned quite often from Rome.

One of the friends whose company I had most looked forward to enjoying in Edinburgh was T. B. Simpson. I quoted in my last Octave from that absorbing diary he kept during the last war and published privately. He had been Sheriff of Caithness, Sutherland, Orkney and Shetland for many years but he had just become Sheriff of Perth and Angus which is regarded as the doyen of Sheriffdoms. Tom Simpson had been at Magdalen some years after me and we had arranged to meet for the Gaudy that summer. However, he was unable to come because he had to go down to the Coronation Naval Review at Spithead about which he wrote me a typically amusing letter.

"How I should have liked to be at that Gaudy! . . . I was conveyed in state to the Naval Review at Spithead in the Lighthouse ship the *Pharos*, sailing from Granton and completed a *periplous* by Land's End and the Isle of Man (where the Northern Lights run the lighthouses) to Ardrossan. . . .

"To return to the *Pharos* voyage . . . these accidents to one of my colleagues and myself had to yield place to what befell Gilchrist (now Sir James) the Sheriff of the Lothians. Overcome by a sudden attack of mal-de-mer he puked his upper dentures over the stern of the *Pharos* and had the mortification of seeing them sink zigzag into the cold waters off St Abbs. He pluckily continued the voyage, subsisting on drink rather than food and was rewarded by finding his spares awaiting him at Portsmouth. . . . This was not the end of Gilchrist's adventures since he was seized with a cramp on the morning after the Review so badly that a funeral at sea seemed likely. In fact I composed his 'Marine Epitaph':

When Sheriff Gilchrist died on board
We buried him off Portland Bill,
But Heaven this bounty did accord,
His teeth remain in Scotland still.

"During the Royal Visit the Secretary of State for Scotland[1] cheered up the Queen on the tiring journey by telling her about G's teeth only to find that she had heard all about it from Philip[2] (Sheriff J. R. not her husband) the day before, including the poem! Philip, who is two inches shorter than me, left the *Pharos* tipping the beam at 18 stone 10. It is said that when H.M. knighted him she said instead of 'Rise, Sir Randall' 'Roll over, Sir Cumference' and that Philip answered in a hurt voice 'But I've rolled over already, your Majesty'."

Tom Simpson was the best after-dinner speaker I have enjoyed listening to; in style and content his speeches were perfect. At the party we had as a kind of house-warming for 31 Drummond Place on my 71st birthday he proposed the toast of many happy returns. Nine months later Tom Simpson was dead, and I still miss his wit, his humour and his kindness.

In that July I received a welcome invitation from Neil Shaw, the Secretary of An Comunn Gaidhealach:

"I am directed by the Jubilee Mod Committee to extend to you a very cordial invitation to preside over the Grand Concert to be held in the Cinema, Oban on 11th October.

"The Members of the Committee have asked to express the hope that you may be able to accept this invitation. . . .

"You will be glad to know that the entries are most encouraging and in the oral section constitute an all-time record."

Chrissie and I stayed with our dearly loved Gillespies at the Columba Hotel and hardly ever got to bed before 4 a.m. from the various ceilidhs we attended. Lord Graham[3] was over from Rhodesia to see his father who was very near his end. It was heartening to find him still as enthusiastic as ever about the Gaelic language.

Another visitor was the Premier of Nova Scotia, Angus Macdonald.[4] He was a Macdonald of Kinloch Moidart and a fluent Gaelic speaker. He made a deep impression on me and I felt that Nova Scotia was indeed lucky to have such a man as leader. For me,

[1] Viscount Stuart of Findhorn.
[2] The late Sir Randall Philip, Q.C.
[3] The 7th Duke of Montrose.
[4] The late Hon. Angus Macdonald, Q.C., LL.D., D.C.L.

that meeting was a link with the '45. I had met the previous year Sister St Veronica of St Francis Xavier University, Antigonish. She was a fervid Scottish Nationalist with an acute intelligence and I am still privileged to be in correspondence with her.

I had taken the chair at another concert in St Andrew's Hall, Glasgow.

"The Celtic Congress is to be held in Glasgow this year from 12th to 18th August and will be attended by delegates from Ireland, Wales, Isle of Man, Cornwall and Brittany."

It was quite an evening with Scottish, Welsh and Irish singers in their own languages, dancers and pipers.

When I was asked at the beginning of the autumn term to address the freshmen of Edinburgh University I did not feel as nervous as I should probably feel today. I could not have had a jollier audience, and I had the pleasure of addressing the freshmen of two more years.

Those students I talked to in 1953, 54 and 55 are now in their thirties; the students who listened (politely) to my Rectorial address at Glasgow University are now in their fifties and sixties. I believe that most of the students of today will move calmly enough into their thirties and fifties.

When these words are published we shall have quitted the sexy 'sixties and entered what I hope will be the sensible 'seventies. Much will depend on whether Television and the Press will display as much moral courage in the 'seventies as the immoral courage they showed in the 'sixties.

Two days before I talked to those freshmen in Edinburgh I had had a painful experience in the south of England.

Toward the end of August Rupert Croft-Cooke had written to me from The Long House, Ticehurst, Sussex:

"Some very hideous circumstances have arisen in my life which I think will best be explained to you by the enclosed memorandum written for my Solicitors and Counsel. I know that you with your hatred for tyrannous methods and victimisation, will feel indignation over this as well as sympathy."

With this letter he sent me the memorandum, the thirty-ninth and last page of which I quote:

"It seems to me that grave constitutional issues are involved here. On an accusation obtained by police coercion from two men awaiting trial for a brutal assault, with no corroborative evidence and without a semblance of truth, I have been taken to gaol at 2.30 a.m., kept there for 30 hours, prevented from communication with my solicitor, insulted and humiliated. Joseph Alexander who is of blameless life and character has been dragged from a sickbed and similarly treated, while Ronald Crawford, a guest in my house, has been assaulted and insulted. My career has been jeopardised and will certainly be most adversely affected even after acquittal.

"I must make it plain that I do not want merely that Counsel shall 'get me off' on this charge; I must have the very fullest vindication and if there is a case for it, compensation. I hope that a Leader may be found for the trial who can show my character and life as they are so that it may be seen how a dirty-minded group of men have believed evil, and done evil to justify their belief."

On 21st September Croft-Cooke wrote to me again:

"It is with the greatest diffidence that I write this letter and I would not do so if my Solicitors and Counsel had not emphasised the necessity for it.

"I want to ask you to give evidence of character for me in the case which is coming up. I know how difficult it must be for you to do this when you are moving house in addition to all your other engagements and work, but it does seem to me that it may make all the difference to my chances of acquittal. There is no one else who both knows me well and is so well known.

"I am told that the outcome is not in any great doubt. As you say, no jury could convict on the evidence of such a pair of young blackguards. Since the events of which you already know they have *both* been in detention for other offences. The legal aid adviser to whom they went is being called by us and will say that he is convinced that they were speaking the truth when they told him that their accusations against me were fabricated, and so on.

"But in this kind of case it seems that evidence of character is regarded as being of the very highest importance and this encourages me to make my request even though I know it must cause inconvenience and trouble to you. Apart from everything else it would greatly ease the strain and doubt I feel now if I knew that you were going to be there.

"The probable date is October 8th or 9th but that is not certain and Counsel might arrange it otherwise if you wish. Will you let me know?"

By the same post a letter came from Croft-Cooke's solicitors and I then replied:

"I shall be able to attend the Court and give evidence for Mr

Croft-Cooke if the case is held on the 7th or 8th October—much preferable for me on the 7th. I have to address the Freshmen at Edinburgh University at 10 o'clock on October 9th, and after that I have a week of public engagements in Scotland. The 7th and the 8th are the only two possible dates because I have public engagements for the whole of the preceding week.

"I have known Mr Croft-Cooke personally for about 20 years, having expressed admiration for his work when I was reviewing for the *Daily Mail*. This was the occasion of our meeting first. He came up to stay with me in Barra in the Outer Hebrides when he was on leave during the war in order to discuss with me intelligence work. I have never had the faintest reason to suppose that he could be involved in such a case as the present one. I know that he has for many years been captivated by the lives of circus folks and gipsies, and I can easily understand that such company might puzzle a small country town. I have been to his house at Ticehurst on one occasion to meet various old literary friends in the neighbourhood. Finally, let me repeat I have had no reason to associate him with this kind of thing, and that if I had I should certainly have warned him very seriously of the folly of keeping bad company. To enjoy low company is quite a different matter."

The other witness to be called was Patrick Kinross.[1] That lovable barrister 'Khaki' Roberts[2] was to lead for the defence, and for some reason the trial was to be conducted by the Recorder of Maidstone, although it was entirely the concern of the Sussex Police. Perhaps the Recorder of Lewes would have been so shocked by the behaviour of the police in his own county that it was felt advisable to hold the case before the Recorder of Maidstone.

Croft-Cooke was still completely happy about the result of his trial when he and I and Patrick Kinross lunched together. I was less happy. I had felt that the manner of the Recorder of Maidstone (R. E. Seaton, Q.C.) to the Recorder of Bristol (G. D. Roberts, Q.C.) was verging upon the insolent and I hoped that if Mr R. E. Seaton, Q.C. was arguing a case before the Recorder of Bristol the latter would remember the attitude of his fellow Recorder and treat him with equal offensiveness.

When I stood in the witness-box and saw those twelve turnip-heads that made up the jury I was completely pessimistic about the verdict. All twelve turnip-heads were obviously not paying the least

----

[1] Lord Kinross.
[2] The late G. D. Roberts, Q.C.

attention to my testimony but were all gaping at the Recorder waiting to hear what verdict he would advise them to give.

The Recorder of Maidstone left the jury in no doubt of what he thought the verdict ought to be. They were influenced accordingly and retired obediently to give a verdict of guilty. That did not surprise me after the summing up. What did surprise and shock me was the sentence of twelve months. Such a sentence seemed to me a flagrant encouragement of outrageous behaviour by the Sussex police and equally flagrant encouragement of two blackguard young naval cooks from Chatham.

Rupert Croft-Cooke wrote a book about his case called *The Verdict of You All*. I advise a reading of it. My own experience with the police prejudiced me in their favour, and I had found it difficult at first not to fancy that Rupert Croft-Cooke was not imagining much of what he wrote in the first thirty-eight pages of that document he had sent me in August. I pressed him hard, but I was completely satisfied that there was in it neither fancy nor exaggeration.

I must make it clear that I have written this account of ill-justice without letting Rupert Croft-Cooke know of my intention. The fact that he himself wrote *The Verdict of You All* absolves me from being blamed for digging up something best forgotten. It will be best forgotten by the Sussex police.

Ten days before I came to the end of my seventy-first year I was down in London to attend the Jubilee Dinner in celebration of the fiftieth anniversary of the founding of Foyle's Bookshop. There were over 200 guests at the Dorchester on that January evening. After the loyal toast Lord Birkett[1] rose to propose Literature which was to be replied to by J. B. Priestley.

Lord Birkett was now generally recognised as the most eloquent and accomplished speaker for an occasion like this. He never used a note but he had obviously considered the matter and form of his speech most carefully. Nevertheless, the effect on an audience was that he was speaking completely impromptu.

For some reason Jack Priestley was feeling annoyed with television that evening, and he opened his speech by wondering why he had been asked to reply to the toast of Literature, seeing that nowadays there was no literature except Harding and Harben. He then went on to complain of the way the bureaucrats were handling the paper problem. I agreed with every word he had said about paper but

[1] The late Rt. Hon. Lord Justice Birkett, Q.C.

felt that the toast of Literature was not the time to talk about the nuisance of paper.

The next toast was to Foyle's Bookshop which I had to give. Luckily for me I could with complete sincerity say how much as an author I owed to Foyle's Bookshop, and therefore faintly emotionalise the atmosphere. The brothers W. A. and Gilbert Foyle replied. They had started their career as booksellers by peddling them from bicycles before they felt inspired in 1904 to acquire and open a bookshop in Charing Cross Road which had grown into the huge storehouse of books which it was fifty years later.

The last toast was to Our Friends in the Trade by Christina Foyle with her usual knowledge of exactly the right thing to say and the right thing to do. Michael Joseph made an excellent reply.

SEVENTY-ONE YEARS OLD: 1954

WE had the first of so many good Edinburgh birthday parties which have clipped the wings of Time's chariot. John Hope-Johnston came up and took on the hard task of arranging my books, and I was back again on the island of Herm over thirty years before when he tackled the same task and made a difficult time seem easy with his perfect conversation. He was ten days older than myself but he had been denied that complete awareness of the present which makes the old age of two other dear octogenarian friends so much part of the present: Martin Secker and Frank Swinnerton.

Lily had been coming to us every weekend while we were settling in at Drummond Place, and now she decided to give up her teaching job in Glasgow and apply for one of the Edinburgh schools. At this date, the Edinburgh Education authorities were short of teachers, and we naturally expected that they would welcome the opportunity of securing the services of an experienced teacher. To my astonishment when she notified the Edinburgh Education authorities of her desire to take up an Edinburgh appointment a ridiculously pompous reply came to say that she would be put on a waiting list and interviewed in due course. I advised her to resign from teaching not only in Glasgow but anywhere else in Scotland. This she did, and a few months later went to London and enrolled at a School of Beauty Culture owned by Mrs Hartley, the mother of Vivien Leigh.

A week after my birthday I was at the 179th anniversary dinner of the Wagering Club. The toast list has almost an eighteenth century air. The Chairman would propose The Queen and then The Duke of Edinburgh, Queen Elizabeth the Queen Mother, The Duke of Rothesay[1] and the other members of the Royal Family. The Croupier (Mr John Cameron, D.F.C., Q.C.)[2] would then propose the Naval, Military and Air Forces of the Commonwealth to which Lieut-General Sir Colin M. Barber, K.C.B., D.S.O., would reply. Then the Chairman would propose The Wagering Club and the Memory of Bain Whyt; the Budget would be proposed by the Chaplain (Mr H. McKechnie, Q.C.). Bets to be Determined would be proposed by the Secretary (Mr C. W. Graham Guest, Q.C.).[3]

[1] H.R.H. Prince Charles.
[2] The Hon. Lord Cameron.
[3] The Hon. Lord Guest.

Finally the Chairman, Croupier, Chaplain and Secretary would be proposed by the Chairman-Elect, Eric Linklater.

This was not an occasion when I could make an impromptu speech and I find the copy of my speech typed out in capitals and I think the story of the Wagering Club curious enough to warrant its record in the Appendix B.

Iain Hamilton, who became assistant editor after Walter Taplin went on to become editor of *The Spectator*, came up to Edinburgh to suggest that I should take over the weekly article which Harold Nicolson had just given up. At first I refused because I felt that every reader of *The Spectator* would be missing Harold Nicolson's *Marginal Comment* so acutely that any successor would inevitably be resented.

However, in the end I agreed to write the weekly article under the title *Sidelight*. Walter Taplin was a very tolerant Editor and Iain Hamilton a very sympathetic Assistant-Editor. About the first *Sidelight* I wrote was to protest against the idiotic bogeyman way in which the Nationalist 'conspirators' were being treated for eliminating the 'Two' after the Queen's initials on pillar-boxes. She was Queen Elizabeth the First of Scotland; she was Queen Elizabeth the Second of England.

I much enjoyed writing those *Sidelights* and the letters I received every week from readers encouraged me to believe that there were still far more sensible people in the world than I was beginning to think. One of the first of those *Spectator* letters came from the great cricketer Pelham Warner:

"I read with some amusement your essay on the use of the word 'literally', the more so as you mentioned the fearful crimes for which my father, Sir Pelham held W. G. Grace responsible."

This was when in a broadcast Sir Pelham Warner observed that W. G. Grace literally killed the fast bowlers of his prime, which, I added, must have given a lot of work to his brother E. M. Grace, the coroner.

"My father asked me to tell you how much he enjoyed reading the essay, and how amused he was by your references to 'the coroner'.

"My reason for writing to you is, that I seem to remember when I was at Eton reading a description of a scene in the House of Commons when Disraeli was making one of his powerful speeches, and Mr Gladstone was alleged to have been so impressed that he 'sat literally glued to the Treasury Bench'.

"Unfortunately I do not remember who made this remark, but

C.M. and Gilbert
Harding at
Aberdeen University,
1953

C.M. recording a
talk with
Gilbert Harding

C.M.'s *This is Your Life*, 1956

C.M., Rose
Macaulay, and
Rosamond
Lehmann, 1954

even if it has to be an unofficial one, I thought you might like to have it for your collection."

I gratefully acknowledged that 'literally', and added another to my collection from the Racing Correspondent who, in discussing the chances of various entries in the St Leger of 1932 reminded his readers that Cameronian had literally run away with the Two Thousand Guineas.

"I have been greatly amused by your collection of 'literallys' of February 5th. I should like to add one to your collection. This will serve as a companion to the one about Cameronian. A Racing Correspondent discussing the prospects for the 1952 St Leger wrote 'Tulyar is literally full of beans'."

I had a dozen more 'literallys' from correspondents but I must be content with quoting those two.

Realms of Silver was published that March and I was working hard to finish *Ben Nevis Goes East* in time for Chatto's to publish in the autumn.

I was elected President of the Croquet Association in succession to Sir Colchester Wemyss. Of the games I can no longer play I miss croquet more than any other. I sometimes wonder if the ousting of croquet from Wimbledon by lawn-tennis was an omen of the continuously more fidgety existence of the twentieth century.

In one of my *Sidelights* at the end of May I made a reference to Evelyn Waugh. He wrote:

I was touched and exhilarated to read the kind reference to myself in your Spectator article.

Thanks awfully.

In a Panorama programme of this month I made some remarks about British roads and paid a tribute to the lorry-drivers who, in spite of such roads, set an example of road manners to bus-drivers and all too many private motorists. Among the letters I received was one from a lorry-driver for which I was grateful:

"I saw you and heard your criticisms in the Television programme, Panorama, and while I endorse fully what you said regarding the Highways of Britain, I would like, as a long-distance driver, to thank you for what you said about us.

"I know that as professional drivers we must by our own behaviour try to improve the standard of driving of other road users, by extending to them every courtesy and assistance that we can, thereby lessening the death and injury rate on the roads.

C

"On Monday next, I shall be leaving myself for Scotland via the Great North Road, the A1 which to me is the longest, dreariest journey that a driver undertakes, what with the tortuous bends beyond Biggleswade and the flat monotonous country, one is rather glad to get into the hills of Scotland, even if it does mean long drags in low gear, at least one's eyelids don't seem quite so heavy.

"So thanking you once again for your kind words, which proved to me that our efforts to be courteous are appreciated by some folks, even though we do exceed a little our legal speed limits, but then we must keep awake!"

In that summer of 1954, the agitation for Enosis or union with Greece was becoming more vociferous, and I wrote a *Sidelight* in *The Spectator* to put the Cypriot point of view which was already being shamefully distorted by the British Press. Nothing yet had been heard of E.O.K.A. and nothing would have been heard of it if the Government had possessed a Minister with common sense to handle the situation in Cyprus. This article brought me letters and telegrams of thanks from Cypriot Associations and individual Cypriots from all over the world. Among them I was naturally much encouraged to receive the following letter:

"Nicosia Cyprus
8th June 1954

Compton Mackenzie Esq.,
    c/o Spectator,
99 Gower Street,
London, W.C.1.

Dear Mr Mackenzie,

We are very grateful for your article, 'Sidelight' in the 'Spectator' which places the Cyprus question on its proper basis and suggests the only rightful solution.

We have always been moved by your articles on various occasions, which are inspired by a warm philhellenic spirit and a genuine liberal attitude of mind. We are particularly gratified by your above mentioned article which effectively refutes groundless arguments put forward for the purpose of denying the right of the people of Cyprus to their national liberty.

Wishes to God.
Makarios
Archbishop of Cyprus Makarios

Two months later I received a letter from Mr Zeno Rasides the
Delegate of the Ethnarchy of Cyprus staying in the Park Lane Hotel:
"Dear Mr Mackenzie,

I wish to convey to you on behalf of His Beatitude the Archbishop
of Cyprus his great appreciation and that of the people of the island
for the valuable contribution to the cause of their national liberty
rendered by your most lucid and forceful articles. . . ."

I should not meet His Beatitude until four years later in Athens
when I shall tell of that meeting later in this Octave. It is bitter to
reflect on the misery caused during those five years by that curious
attraction the Turks have for so many British statesmen and
soldiers. The Tory Press encouraged this Turkish obsession. *The
Scotsman* went so far as to print a letter from some jackass pleading
for us to expel all Greeks from Cyprus. Perhaps the outrageous
treatment of the Catholic minority in the Six Counties made the
Tory Press so tenderly concerned for the much smaller Turkish minority in Cyprus: Ulster may have lain heavily upon their conscience.

In a less controversial *Sidelight* I told of seeing the planet Venus
by daylight at Capri and of thinking at first it was an aeroplane. I
had a fascinating letter from a Commander at the Admiralty:

"During the Spring of 1937 I was a Midshipman in the battleship
'Royal Oak' engaged on the Spanish Patrol in the Mediterranean
with another 'R' Class Battleship, the 'Royal Sovereign', I think,
and was engaged in a practice shoot during the forenoon. I was
Snotty of the Watch on the bridge at the time. Suddenly three or
four large columns of water shot up a short distance ahead of us.
I remember thinking that the 'Royal Sovereign's' marksmanship
must be pretty poor, when I looked up and saw two aeroplanes
flying off into the blue. We had in fact been attacked quite unexpectedly and in earnest by some ill-disposed, or perhaps misinformed,
individual.

"As a result of this attack we closed up the high-angle guns-crews
for the rest of the day. That afternoon the alarm was given, and sure
enough there, high in the sky, was a bright silvery plane glistening
in the sunlight. The high-angle armament was loaded and brought
to bear on the target whilst we all waited to see whether this plane
too might prove hostile. The moments slipped by, silence fell and
the tension rose. The plane, however, appeared to keep at extreme
range—shadowing no doubt. There were some sheepish faces a few
moments later when the Navigator had to admit that the 'enemy
plane' was in fact Venus."

Pressure may have been brought on *The Spectator* not to use any more of my Cyprus *Sidelights*. Anyway, just before I was leaving for a fortnight in Denmark arranged for me by the Danish Institute, the editor wrote to say he had to make one or two cuts. "I had it in mind to use your article if I possibly could so as to spare you the labour of having to write another one during your Danish trip. Enjoy yourself." What a model of editorial manners!

My last job before setting sail from Leith to Denmark was for the 'Honest Toun's' Association of Musselburgh, which considered itself a senior 'burgh' to Edinburgh and likely to remain a 'burgh' when Edinburgh had ceased to exist or become a suburb of London. My job was to perform the Sashing Ceremony on the banks of the Esk. I should unsash the Honest Lad and Lass of 1953 with thanks for their services and then I should charge and sash the Honest Lad and Lass of 1954. It was a fine July evening and all went well.

The M.S. *Gullfoss* of 4000 tons called at Leith on the way to and from Reykjavik and Copenhagen. I had a splendid ten days and met a large number of delightful people but as I look back on those ten days I cannot disentangle them and I shall not attempt to record my impressions in detail. I came back to Scotland thinking how much more Denmark had made of her resources than we had and wondering if even yet Scotland could detach itself from London and become another Denmark. I sailed back to Leith in the much smaller *S.S. Horsa*.

I went for a day or two to Stratford and attended a performance of *Troilus and Cressida* at the Memorial Theatre. It was the first time I had seen a performance of *Troilus and Cressida* and I waited with faint anxiety for the curtain to go up in case I was going to be given a demonstration of how to bring Shakespeare to life in the second half of the twentieth century. I was pleasantly surprised. The performance was a delight, and I wrote an enthusiastic *Sidelight* about it.

Glen Byam Shaw, the director, took the trouble to send me a welcome 'thank you' and I was glad I had been able to communicate my pleasure and admiration:

The fact that you approve of my production has meant more to me than anything else either good or bad that has been written about the presentation of the play.

Not only did Byam Shaw send me a 'thank you' but Anthony Quayle, who had given a performance of Pandarus I still recall, also sent me a 'thank you':

It would be hard to tell you what pleasure and encouragement your words have given to us who work in this theatre.

He went on to say what actors thought of dramatic critics. It was exactly what I thought. Many dramatic critics are able to judge a play, usually with the help of other dramatic critics during the first interval. Hardly any dramatic critics are able to recognise what is a difficult part to play and what is an easy one. The company at Stratford-on-Avon realised that I did know the difference between a difficult and an easy part.

About this time the Beaverbrook Press were indulging in a campaign to prevent Lord Mountbatten's being made First Sea Lord. He was now Commander-in-Chief, Mediterranean. I knew that this had been his ambition since, when as a boy at Dartmouth, he had had to read the campaign in the *Daily Mail* to force his father Prince Louis of Battenburg[1] to resign from his post as First Sea Lord. Lord Mountbatten had enjoyed almost every great post one man could attain in his own lifetime, but he had not yet been First Sea Lord. I wrote a *Sidelight* in *The Spectator* and recall winding up by saying as an answer to the criticism of his socialistic tendencies that he was about as red as the Admiral of the Red in the days of Lord Nelson.

I was naturally greatly pleased to receive a letter in his own hand from Commander-in-Chief, Mediterranean, written on September 6th:

My dear Compton Mackenzie,

So many of my friends have sent me a copy of your article in the Spectator saying 'at last someone is standing up to Beaverbrook on your behalf' that I felt I could not let this pass without letting you know how much Edwina and I appreciate your article.

We used to be great friends from 1924–1942 but then apparently on some personal grounds he informed me he would now regard me as his enemy and I have never really got to the bottom of the reason.

However, as a serving Naval Officer, his vendetta does not do me any harm, perhaps almost the contrary! But that does not mean to say that I do not appreciate very much indeed the spirit in which you wrote that nice article.

Yours ever
Mountbatten of Burma

I wrote back to say that I attributed Beaverbrook's vendetta to Noel Coward's film *In Which We Serve* for which Lord Louis Mountbatten had given Coward some valuable coaching to avoid making

[1] The 1st Marquis of Milford Haven.

Naval gaffes. The film opened with a copy of the *Daily Express* of September 2nd, 1939, floating across Portsmouth Harbour. In banner headlines on the front page was THERE WILL BE NO WAR.

The mortification that headline must have meant to Beaverbrook at the time was still mortifying twelve years later.

In that October I performed as difficult a job as I ever took on. The London County Council after resisting for some time had finally surrendered to the continuous prodding by the Wilde Centenary Committee and had agreed that a plaque should be put up on the house in Tite Street, Chelsea, where the 'wit and dramatist' of that plaque had been living at the time of the disaster that befell him.

It had been hoped that Max Beerbohm would be able to make the journey from Rapallo in order to perform the unveiling. Unfortunately Max's health forbade the journey and he sent instead a written tribute to Oscar Wilde.

Vyvyan Holland asked me to read Max Beerbohm's tribute and make a speech before the unveiling and later to attend a lunch at the Savoy to read other tributes and make another speech myself.

At first I refused. I had not known Wilde and people might resent my being asked to do the unveiling:

"You knew Robbie Ross, Reggie Turner and Bosie Douglas."

"I think myself, Vyvyan, that you are the one who should do the actual unveiling and make the speech."

"Nothing will induce me to," Vyvyan firmly declared.

At last I gave way and agreed to perform. I was nervous beforehand about my task, but when I saw Tite Street packed with people and immediately opposite, the windows of the Victoria Hospital for Children packed with nurses I nearly gave way to something which I had never experienced and that was stage fright. Montgomery Hyde, then an Ulster M.P., was in the Chair and the Mayor of Chelsea was on the platform which had been rigged up. Just as I was going to speak I caught sight of T. S. Eliot wheeling along John Hayward in his invalid chair. For some reason this made me more nervous than ever. We had heard that they were expecting protests in Dublin when the plaque on the house in which Wilde was born would be unveiled by Lennox Robinson, and I prayed that there would not be any protests in London. No open air audience could have been more sympathetic than that audience in Tite Street. Nevertheless, I was wondering whether the sympathy was for what I felt must be very obvious nervousness or whether they really had been moved by what I said. The first person to congratulate me was Tom Eliot and I was gratified indeed by the warmth of his praise.

It was reassuring to read in the *Irish Times*:

"Sir Compton Mackenzie did the unveiling to perfection, to everyone's absolute satisfaction . . .

"He turned to the house where they had held the public auction. He remembered the last two items on the list: 'one box of children's toys'; 'one rabbit hutch'. Here I thought Sir Compton was not going to be able to proceed, but he did, and the unveiling was greeted with wet eyes as well as loud cheers."

With Vyvyan Holland standing by me, one of those two little boys to whom that box of toys belonged, I could not for a moment or two speak.

The report of the centenary commemoration in the *Manchester Guardian* of October 18th is such a model of good journalism that I feel it should be preserved, and so it may be read in Appendix D.

With one exception the Press commented favourably on the ceremony. That exception was Peterborough's column in the *Daily Telegraph*:

"NO INSPIRATION FOR WILDE

"A correspondent who attended the unveiling of the Oscar Wilde plaque in Tite Street is indignant about the event. He tells me he has seldom been to a duller or less uninspiring performance.

"Sir Compton Mackenzie who performed the ceremony had never seen Wilde. My correspondent says that his address lacked spontaneity—he might have been reading a proclamation.

"Of the various people who might have been asked to unveil the plaque he mentioned Mr Holland, Wilde's surviving son—who was there but was not even invited to speak."

I wrote to 'Peterborough':

"On October 15th, the day before the unveiling of the Oscar Wilde plaque, I was told that there was likely to be an offensive reference to it in the Peterborough column. Therefore I find it a curious coincidence that a correspondent should have been able next day to provide you with the required offensiveness. You may be able to offer a satisfactory explanation, and so spare me the necessity of writing to your Editor. . . .

"For your guidance it was Vyvyan Holland who asked me to unveil the plaque . . . I commend to your attention the account of the ceremony in the Manchester Guardian as an example of honest and efficient journalism, and I await your reply . . ."

'Peterborough' wrote back to say he could not accept responsibility for words written in Chelsea before he returned from Moscow. Then the Editor of the *Daily Telegraph* wrote on October 21st:

"Your letter of the 20th to 'Peterborough' was, of course, brought straight to me. I find it at once distressing and extraordinary.

"I do not know who was the psychic individual who was able to forecast what would appear in Peterborough. He must have remarkable powers because it had not been decided to have a paragraph at all until after the ceremony. . . .

"You have, I think, been a journalist yourself, and a very good one. You must therefore know that in matters of this kind what is really dishonest is the alteration of the impression of somebody who was present by somebody who was not. I am indeed sorry if the impressions of this particular person were not agreeable to you, and more than sorry if they did you an injustice. I cannot correct the impressions, but I am very willing to put right any errors of fact, whether stated or implied. They seem to me to be confined to the circumstances owing to which you spoke and Mr Vyvyan Holland did not; and if you would care to write me a letter of correction I will be glad to publish it."

I wrote back:

"I shall not send you a letter of correction. With such tenderness for your correspondent's feelings you might suspect that I should have as much tenderness for Vyvyan Holland's. Moreover, I do not wish to lend undue importance to a gossip paragraph in *The Daily Telegraph* when the facts have been reported with dignity and accuracy by *The Times* and *The Manchester Guardian* and when the *only* sneer throughout the Press was provided by your paper. Presumably this was editorial policy and the curious coincidence becomes even more curious."

I wound up with another note to 'Peterborough':

"It was a vicious paragraph because it was obviously intended to wound Vyvyan Holland, who is a dear friend of mine. If your Editor supposes that I should have bothered to make any fuss on my own account he must be strangely *ingenu* for a seasoned journalist."

The recognition of Oscar Wilde's centenary by the L.C.C. seemed almost like an effort to atone for the many acts of vandalism it had committed. Yet if the Vandals showed a faint trace of civilisation the Philistines were on the warpath again. I had been much shaken by the behaviour of both the Bench and of the police in the Croft-Cooke case; it seemed to me that the celebration of the Wilde

Centenary had stirred up Philistine opinion to denounce the suggestion that the government should appoint a committee of enquiry into the argument that homosexuality among people of age should cease to be a penal offence. I wrote an article strongly critical of the judicial attitude that was becoming more prevalent.

In that November I had written a *Sidelight* about Max Beerbohm in *The Spectator* and a mutual friend wrote from Italy to tell me about Max: "He is as puckish as ever but getting very feeble". Then he went on:

"I applaud the courage of your protest against our iniquitous interpretation of 'justice' regarding those appalling homosexual cases. What cowards we are! I see that the Committee appointed to make an 'enquiry' has been unable to get a single distinguished member; and I really don't see how any enquiry can be of any avail unless they get one, at least, 'Homo' on to the Committee who really knows what they will be talking about! But in the present climate of opinion, no one would be forthcoming, either off or on the committee, to say anything. Meanwhile we have an outrageous example in this last six months. Mr Justice X, who showed himself to be a man of sense on the subject of obscene literature, is nevertheless of a backward mentality, it would seem. Last June, in the Midlands, he sentenced a wretched youth who had hung around bars, to three years imprisonment, and on sentencing him said 'Your crime is worse than murder'!!

"Last week at the —— Assizes Mr Justice X sentenced a youth of 19 to a mere 18 months, saying 'You took this girl into the wood, you assaulted her in the most violent fashion, terrified the life out of her and pretended you were going to murder her.' He seduced the girl, 16 years old, by forcible assault and pleaded guilty to carnal knowledge of her. I should have thought that all this was, if not 'worse than murder' and merely an attempt at it, a case for three years.

"In this week's Spectator Angus Wilson has a letter suggesting a home for medical treatment of homosexuals. What rubbish! There is *no cure* and every psychologist I have ever come across on these cases is largely a charlatan. What we want is a 'home' or training institute for our judges like X; a revision of the law in sex cases; with ample provision for the protection of juveniles. I think every judge should be sentenced to reading Vyvyan Holland's very moving story."

I had been impelled to use my pen to get that preposterous clause

in the Criminal Law Amendments Act of 1886 amended after I was
told by a Treasury Counsel that he estimated the cause of three-
quarters of male suicides was due to blackmail or fear of scandal.
I am glad to have lived long enough to see the reform of that penal
clause. It should be realised that some of those who tried hardest
in both Houses of Parliament to prevent that reform were themselves temperamental homosexuals who had successfully resisted
the desire to give way to their temperament and were therefore
determined to make it as unpleasant as possible for those who had
succumbed.

The situation in Cyprus was worrying. Harold Nicolson and I
were both co-opted into a Parliamentary Committee of Labour
members who feared that the way in which the Government was
handling the situation would provoke instead of allay the threat
of violence.

I find a document headed 'This document is the property of Her
Britannic Majesty's Government. It was sent to Sir Compton
Mackenzie with the compliments of the Under-Secretary of State
for Foreign Affairs.'

"Speech made by the Minister of State in the General Committee
of the United Nations on the Inscription of the Cyprus item on
September 23 1954."

It was not an encouraging exposition of British reasons for the
refusal of Enosis or Union with Hellas, and it was clear to me that
this British Government would make the same mess of the Levant
as had been made by successive governments for the last fifty
years.

With an apologetic pen I quote the fly-blown rhetoric with which
the Minister of State concluded his speech:

"We envy Greece the glories of her past and the treasures and
beauties of her art and literature. It hurts to differ on a matter about
which strong feelings are held. I assure you there is nothing anti-
Greek in our attitude. We stand by what we believe to be in the
interests of our two countries and the free world. We will do all we
can, for our part, to see that this disagreement raises no bitterness
and leaves no scars."

In that October when that Parliamentary Committee was trying
to avert violence in Cyprus, the Society of Authors attained its 70th
birthday. The occasion was celebrated by a great reception and
dinner at the Dorchester. John Masefield was too frail to stand the

strain of such a function and I was asked by Osbert Sitwell, Chairman of the Management Committee, and Denys Kilham Roberts, the Secretary, to deputise for the President with Rosamond Lehmann as the ceremonial hostess. It was a splendid evening. Instead of the usual way tables are arranged for a big dinner there was no high table but a lot of oval tables all over the room, each sitting about a dozen members and guests. Anthony Gilkes, the new High Master of St Paul's, was at my table. His father had been a great Headmaster of Dulwich when I was at St Paul's. I found Gilkes delightful company and felt that contemporary Paulines were to be congratulated. We had several speeches from the various tables, of which the two best came from Arthur Bliss[1] and Alan Herbert.[2]

At the end of the month I had the pleasure of attending the Wexford Festival. It was opened by Lord Killanin and the opera was *La Sonnambula* with three exquisite Bellini arias. The Wexford Festival could now be considered an undoubted success. The Town Council had extended their illuminations.

It was this year that the first Festival Forum was held in the Cinema Palace during which there were one or two moments when I almost emulated the sleepwalking of the soprano at the Theatre Royal. One sat up very late every night at Wexford. I am a bit muddled which year the various members of the Forum answered the questions sent in by the audience, but I know that Edward Longford[3] was one of the members of the Forum this year. Edward Longford was a man for whose moral courage I had a very high regard. He stood up for the cause of a free Ireland with complete integrity of purpose and behaviour. The southern Irish were so astonished at the support they were given by a member of the old Ascendancy that at first they could not believe his support was genuine. However, they would learn and appreciate how genuine it was.

Christine Longford wrote two or three novels which I was able to salute enthusiastically when I was reviewing for the *Daily Mail*. However, to support her husband's enthusiasm for drama she turned away from novels to write plays for the Gate Theatre. If any publisher reads these words of mine (which is most unlikely) he would do well to take my advice and get hold of those early novels of Christine Longford.

---

[1] Sir Arthur Bliss, Master of the Queen's Music.
[2] Sir Alan Herbert, C.H., President of the Society of Authors.
[3] The late 6th Earl of Longford.

SEVENTY-TWO YEARS OLD: 1955

MY seventy-second birthday party was saddened for me by the absence of Tom Simpson who had died three months before. With few friends have I enjoyed such stimulating conversation and one of the pleasures I had most looked forward to from life in Edinburgh was these talks with Tom Simpson.

Another friend in Edinburgh whose conversation was not at all stimulating went to live on the Riviera, and I wrote to Willie Maugham asking him to be kind to that new resident. Here is Willie's reply from the Villa Mauresque:

"My dear Monty,
Thank you for writing to me. I will get in touch with X—— Y——, and if he is as great a bore as they tell me, all is over between you and me.

Yours ever,
W.S.M."

The Spectator had just been bought by Ian Gilmour and I was not surprised to hear from him:

"I am afraid that owing to the various changes that are being made it will be necessary for *Sidelight* to be written in the office. I understand that because of your very many other commitments, this may be something of a relief to you. . . .

"Needless to say we are extremely grateful to you for all that you have done for *The Spectator*, and I very much hope that we shall still see your name in our columns from time to time. Of course we are going to publish all the *Sidelights* we have in stock. . . ."

In fact I was relieved to be quit of the responsibility for that weekly article but, like Harold Nicolson when he gave up *Marginal Comment*, there would be moments when we should regret not having an opportunity to make a *Marginal Comment* in his case or turn a *Sidelight* in mine upon something we deplored. At the beginning of 1955 for me it was what I considered the fatuous way in which the British Government was handling the situation in Cyprus, culminating this March in the new Colonial Secretary's[1] banishing Archbishop Makarios to the Seychelles. The way in which we were handling Cyprus was exasperating throughout this year. The comments in

[1] Rt. Hon. Viscount Boyd of Merton, C.H.

most of the British Press were contemptible. I think it was in September that *Time and Tide* admonished me, and I wrote the following letter to relieve my exasperation:

"You say I can do nothing more on the Greeks' behalf than complain about the attitude of some British newspapers towards Greece. I should be grateful for advice from you how at the age of 72 I am to pierce a dense conglobulation of stupidity with a pen which is now inevitably a little blunted: I am not romantic enough to suppose that my sword would be of any use.

"However, I beg you will give me a little space for that blunted pen.

"In 1570 the Turks drove the Venetians from Cyprus with the usual Turkish accompaniment of massacre on a grand scale. 20,000 of the inhabitants of Nicosia were put to the sword. Famagusta held out for a year and the Turks as usual violated the terms of capitulation, the Venetian Governor being put to death with horrible torments. Apart from an insurrection in 1764 the three centuries of the Turkish occupation were stagnant.

"In 1878 Disraeli leased the island and another thirty-three years of stagnation ensued. Then Sir John Myres commented in the eleventh edition of the Encyclopaedia Britannica:

"'The Turks and the British have added little, destroyed much, converting churches into mosques and grain-stores, and quarrying walls and buildings in Famagusta.'

"In 1914 when Turkey entered the First War Cyprus was annexed. A year later it was offered to Greece if the Greek army would sacrifice itself in a hopeless attempt to help the Serbs: the offer was refused. Since then Cyprus has had to endure the stuffy administration of the Colonial Office. In 1931 the Governor's residence was burnt, ironically the residence of Sir Ronald Storrs, the only Governor who genuinely loved the island. Enosis with Greece has been ardently desired ever since Greece achieved independence.

"If Cyprus had been granted Union with Greece we should now have all the bases we needed on the island for as long as we wanted to retain them. Moreover, we should have the gratitude, affection and passionate loyalty of every Greek all over the world. Of this my discredited head is as sure as my complimented heart.

"You ask me, sir, if I have read any of the monitorings of the Athens Radio. Can you not make allowances for the bitterness that Greeks feel today when they look back to suffering that was entirely due to their defiance of the Axis, as a reward for which the nation they loved best turns away from them to lick the boots of Turks? Does it not encourage the Athens Radio to be soft-spoken when part of the British Press dares to accuse Greece of ingratitude?

"When Hitler decided to rescue Mussolini in April 1941 we sent an expeditionary force which failed to stop him and added one more to our chronicle of notable retreats and evacuations. For what was Greece to be grateful? A gesture: that is all. Were I indeed romantic I should be able to admire the emotional cartoons now appearing in our Press. Being a realist I find them nauseous.

"Let us be honest with ourselves. We hope to revive the Ottoman Empire to protect us against Russia, and make the Egyptians regret that they turned us out and help us to recover our prestige in the Middle East. Is it surprising that Mr Georgandas has begun to wonder on which side of the Iron Curtain are there more guarantees of freedom and security for Greece? Must we be greatly concerned over the proposed ostracism of Lord Montgomery? Themistocles Aristides, Venizelos, and King Constantine all endured it.

"Gladstone! thou shouldst be living at this hour: England hath need of thee.

Your obedient servant"

That January was made memorable for me by the beginning of my association with Grant's whisky—Standfast and Glenfiddich. From the great advertising firm of Mather and Crowther came a letter which began:

"We are writing to ask you if you would consider sponsoring a series of advertisements for Grant's whisky. . . ."

Mather and Crowther suggested that I should do a series of advertisements with friends of my choosing. These appeared in various newspapers and magazines.

Mather and Crowther wrote:

"We have received a number of bouquets . . . and we would certainly like to thank you for becoming, as it were, the resident host of the series."

Among those who took part in those interviews were Sir William Hutchison, Ivor Brown and Eric Linklater.

Before those interviews in Press advertisements, Alan Herbert, Michael Ayrton and myself, had been photographed by Independent Television sipping a dram of Standfast. However, the Distillers Company had agreed to ban all whisky advertising on TV and of course Grant's had to comply.

Later on this year Grants asked if I could testify exclusively to the merit of Standfast. I could give that testimony with complete sincerity because I had been impressed by the quality of Standfast when I first tasted it among the Whisky Galore in the wrecked S.S. *Politician*. Thus began a happy association with Grants which is still close as I write these words.

When I was living in Barra I used to receive fairly often letters from fervid Protestants denouncing my Popery. All were anonymous and most of them obscene. When I went to live in Edinburgh I expected to receive many more letters denouncing my Popery. Few statements have given me as much satisfaction to make in any article or book I have written as to be able to say that since I came to Edinburgh in 1953 I have not received one anonymous letter from an indignant Protestant, not even one pip from an Orangeman. Without any doubt the Edinburgh of today is much more tolerant than it used to be. Today creatures like Mr Paisley and Pastor Glass seem like characters out of Dickens' novel *Barnaby Rudge*. The advertisement of them by Television and the Press is surely typical of their permissive attitude to the 'permissive society'.

I did receive quite a few anonymous letters from teetotallers reproving me for encouraging the youth of Scotland to drink whisky. The fanaticism of teetotallers and non-smokers is enjoyed by the fanatics because they dislike the taste of alcoholic liquor and even the very smell of tobacco. What worries me about the campaign by non-smoking doctors against tobacco is their failure to bring home to the public that inhaling tobacco is the threat to health not smoking it. What worries me more than the increase of lung cancer is the mental and moral effect of taking drugs. That seems to me a much greater threat to youth's future. I was shocked to read some of the names in that full page advertisement in *The Times* to plead that hashish was physically harmless. It is as well to recall the derivation of 'assassin' both in English and in French. During the Third Crusade, which was the last time the English and the French fought as close allies until the British and French fought as allies in the Crimea, there was a sinister Moslem figure known as the Old Man of the Mountains. It was his habit to ply young Moslems with hashish in order to get them to murder Christians. Assassins were originally hashish eaters.

When Malcolm Muggeridge again condemned drugs during his sermon at St Giles at the opening of the Edinburgh Festival of 1969 several people old enough to know better but wanting to seem young wrote absurd letters to *The Scotsman*. The victim of lung cancer from inhaling tobacco hurts only himself; the cancer of the mind that can come from smoking hashish hurts other people.

When John Partridge who was Secretary of the Imperial Tobacco Company suggested I should write a history of tobacco I was greatly taken with the notion and welcomed the help he offered. I took Byron's epithet and proposed to call my history *Sublime Tobacco*. Imperial Tobacco promised me all possible help, and in June I was writing to tell John Partridge that I should expect to be able to have the book ready for my publishers in time for them to publish *Sublime Tobacco* in the autumn of next year. In June I was writing:

"May I say how very much I appreciate the confidence which your Company has shown in me, and I can assure you that I look forward to writing the book as much as a labour of love as of duty."

I certainly did enjoy the research for *Sublime Tobacco*, and I am always gratified when two or three times a year even now I get letters about *Sublime Tobacco*.

Gilbert Harding had been seriously ill and I must have written to say how glad I was to have good news of his recovery because I find a note from him written that March:

"Dear, dear Monty,

Of course I must answer your kind letter—even if only to say that mid-May should find me restored to a modicum of health, back from a holiday in the sunshine—and of course longing to see you.

My dear love ever

Gilbert"

It must have been my last *Sidelight* about which Rex Warner wrote to me that February. It was one more plea for us to understand the desire of the Cypriots for Union or Enosis with Hellas:

How glad I am that you write! I thought that your article in this week's 'Spectator' was admirable. But how appalling that there weren't a hundred articles everywhere making the same noise! I myself have written to the 'Spectator' and to the 'Times' on the Enosis business—probably in too impulsive language. Anyway my letters were not printed. But I thought that your piece this week was wholly admirable in its restraint and in its overwhelming effect. What is really disturbing (apart from Greece altogether) is that there are so few people who can, as you can, get hold of the public ear at all for talking plain sense and plain decency. . . .

Alas, that piece was not overwhelming enough to stop that idiotic banishment of Archbishop Makarios to the Seychelles.

C.M. signing copies of *Rockets Galore*

C.M. by the Spirit of Hellas at Missolonghi

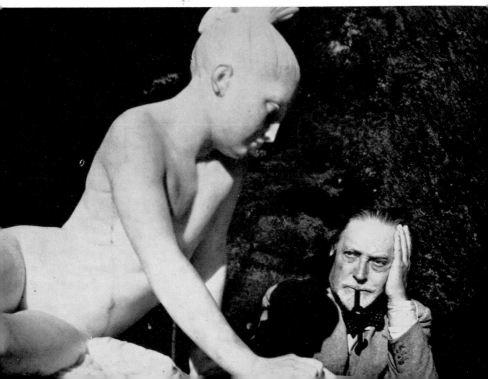

C.M. and Chrissie at the party given by Chatto's at Carpenters' Hall

C.M. in the "Goodbye Piccadilly" programme at the Café Royale

Readers of earlier Octaves will realise what a loss it was to me when John Macpherson, or more familiarly, the Coddie, left us. He was so much a part of Barra, so much a part of my life there, that I felt as if the island itself had floated away like St Brendan's isle. I was able to pay the Coddie a tribute on the radio, and on March 6th Mrs Macpherson wrote to me:

Thank you so very much for your letter and for your wonderful tribute to Coddie on the radio. I need not say how touched we all were and how honoured.

How he would have loved to hear it himself. He spoke of you so often even up to his last days. It will be a long time before we can get used to the sad change in our household.

He had a very happy and peaceful death. May he rest in peace.

With much love from us all.

Yours affectionately

John Campbell collected in a fascinating little volume tales of the Coddie.

Jock Cameron,[1] one of my dearest friends, who was Dean of the Faculty of Advocates, had recently been knighted, and the Scottish Arts Club gave him a dinner, at which I had the privilege of proposing the toast to his health. A year later saw the end of his brilliant advocacy and he became a judge. 'Bill' Hutchison,[2] President of the Royal Scottish Academy, was also at that jolly dinner and replied to the toast to the Arts. Bill and I enjoy (at any rate I do and I hope he did) being occasionally mistaken for one another. He had taken me as his guest to the annual dinner of the Nomads Club in Glasgow of which he was the Honorary President in succession to old Lord Home. It is the job of the Honorary President to find a guest each year who can make a reasonably good speech in reply to his own on some Latin tag. The Nomads Club was founded in 1895 as a kind of Field Club, when its members set out from time to time to explore the countryside near Glasgow. During the winter papers were read by the members, and if a member failed to attend more than two papers running he ceased to be a Nomad.

Bill Hutchison, who would soon resign his Honorary Presidency, being now so busily engaged with his portrait painting in London where he had a studio, was contemplating giving up his beautiful

---

[1] The Hon. Lord Cameron.
[2] The late Sir William Hutchison.

house and studio in Eglinton Crescent. When Bill Hutchison resigned I was elected Honorary President.

I find a good description of that annual dinner of the Nomads in a letter from the President to notify me of the date of the dinner next year.

"Do you think that from your innumerable friends, outstanding in so many spheres of activity, you could entice one or two to come with you to our Dinner? As you may recall from your previous visit to our Club, we are somewhat unorthodox ourselves and we endeavour to keep our Dinner off the stereotyped lines of so many. Indeed, our guests maintain—and we think ourselves—that it is quite the most enjoyable function held in Glasgow!"

I am proud to record that as I write these words in 1969 I am still the Honorary President of the Nomads. Those annual Dinners, of which I have been able to attend all except one since 1956, are always completely enjoyable. They are held in the St Enoch Hotel, Glasgow, and the chef provides the best public dinner I eat anywhere. The Club itself is a small one but each member brings several guests and usually over a hundred sit down to eat that delicious dinner, which deserves to be followed by good speeches and always is. I think that the microphone has been a disadvantage to acting in the theatre but what a blessing it has been for after dinner speakers and their audiences.

In that summer James Thurber came to Scotland to investigate the Loch Ness Monster. We spent two grand evenings in Drummond Place. Helen Thurber, his delightful wife, told him that it was four o'clock when it was really only two o'clock. James was indignant about this, and with my encouragement, planned to stay until four o'clock at the second visit. However, Helen was too clever for us. Alas, I had only those two evenings and another next year with him in London. I found his talk as fascinating as his drawings, and I cherish the letter he sent me after he left Edinburgh. The courage with which James Thurber bore his complete blindness was for me a great example, and I resolved then that if I ever did go completely blind I would try to be as brave as him.

"Hotel Stafford,
St James's Place,
London, S.W.1.
13th August, 1955.

Dear Monty Mackenzie,

"We have been telling everyone since we left Edinburgh of our

two enjoyable evenings at your house, and we shall go on remembering them fondly, and hope to see you again next year.

"I have just sent on to The New Yorker a piece I wrote called
'The Moribundant Life, or Grow Old Along with Whom?', which
deals with the wonderful longevity of writers over here, and our
comparatively short span in America. You are mentioned in it with
wonder and affection, and Helen joins me in repeating the sincere
wish that you may go on forever.

"We are leaving for Paris on Tuesday, where we shall be at the
Hotel Continental until some time in October.

"I am glad that you and Thornton Wilder will by this time have
met. I heard him discussing the theatre on the B.B.C. last Sunday,
which he did with skill and wisdom. I hope he had the chance to
hear you do that imitation of Wordsworth, among other things.

"Since I am an American, it may be that the flame descends,
but I am by no means ready to depart, either this life or these Isles.

"Once more, our combined thanks, best wishes and high regards.
Cordially yours,
James Thurber."

I found the visit from Thornton Wilder less exhilarating because
we had to talk seriously all the time, and I should never have dreamt
of telling my Wordsworth story to him as Thurber hoped I would.
The joy of Thurber's company was the way his blindness was
lighted by his sense of humour. And never for a moment was there
a sign of self-conscious 'funniment' in which he was trying to justify
his reputation for being funny. I could not help feeling that Thornton
Wilder was being careful all the time not to let one suppose he was
ever unaware for a moment of his solemn approach to American
literature. I think that my only experience of an electric razor soon
after this would have amused James Thurber much more than
Thornton Wilder.

A party was given at the Dorchester by a famous razor company
at which various well-known bearded guests were to watch the
beards of three volunteers shaved off by electric razor. Among those
beards in the audience would be Augustus John, Stanley Unwin
and James Robertson Justice.

When I got back to Edinburgh with the complimentary razor I
decided to see if I could make it work. I am clumsy with my fingers
and felt that for me an electric razor might not be a safety razor.
How right I was! I thought at first it sounded like a swarm of bees

in anger and was not surprised when the lobe of my left ear was stung. Then apparently I did something which fused all the lights in 31 Drummond Place. I put that electric razor down and never picked it up again or any other electric razor.

One of the sad losses for which I commiserate with the young TV viewers of today is that they have never watched a magical performance by Ruth Draper. In my novel *Sylvia Scarlett* Sylvia gets the idea of using her adventures all over Europe and South America in performing various scenes in which she plays all the characters, in other words do exactly what Ruth Draper began to do in the United States about the time that *Sylvia Scarlett* was first published. People used to write to me and ask if Sylvia Scarlett was a portrait of Ruth Draper and at the same time other people were writing to ask Ruth Draper if she had got her idea for her impersonations from *Sylvia Scarlett*.

I did not have the pleasure of meeting her for a long time but in this summer she visited Edinburgh and we met for the second time. I find a letter from a great artist which I kept in my archives:

How kind of you to send me the lovely roses with such a nice message. I shall keep it in my archives as a tribute from a great writer who conceived the same idea as I had!

We talked about Henry James of whom she spoke with great affection. Peter Ustinov today has the same art of evocation as Ruth Draper.

I did not attend the Wexford Festival this year because I was rather exhausted after the Cheltenham Literary Festival, the two impresarios of which were John Moore and Robert Henriques. I stayed with Robert and his lovable wife Vi at their farm near Cirencester. Robert Henriques had too many interests. I once said to him, "Robert, you must make up your mind which you want to be considered, a soldier, a novelist, a farmer or an Israeli politician." He had retired as a regular officer in the Royal Artillery before the Second World War to take up farming but rejoined the forces in 1939, fought well in the Desert and wrote one very good novel about the Desert campaign. Then he went back to farming but was out in Israel and a soldier again at the time of the Suez mess.

In a way Robert remained an amateur throughout his life in spite of being a professional soldier, a professional novelist and a professional farmer. He fought his battles hard, whether they were military, literary or agricultural, but he was completely devoid of jealousy and always generous. There were one or two sticky moments during that week of the Festival but I should not be as generous as Robert if I recalled them. Apparently I was able to smooth some of those sticky moments and here is a typically warm pat on the back from Robert in a letter from Winson Mill Farm:

"You made an enormous impression on a very large number of people, all of whom were vastly stimulated by meeting you in private and listening to you in public, and all of whom now feel an immense personal affection."

In fact the hero of that Literary Festival was John Moore, who had a task that only a man of good will like him could have sustained. To me he wrote:

You were wonderful. You were yourself. Bless you, dear Monty, from Robert and Lucile and me and all of us. My only sorrow was I was so very busy I saw so little of you!

As I approach the end of *My Life and Times* I find myself more and more inclined to linger over friends I shall never see again. When I mentioned just now that Robert Henriques had been in the Suez mess there returned to me the picture of Colonel Robert Henriques, R.A., M.B.E., arguing with Lieutenant-Commander David Keir, M.B.E., whether the War Office or the Admiralty were more to blame over Suez. John Moore comes into the Savile Sandpit; soldier and sailor both appeal to him as an airman for a neutral opinion.

"Well," says John Moore, "I think the War Office and the Admiralty made an equal mess."

None of those three close friends shall I see again.

Another friend no longer with us was Leo Robertson whose book about my work had been published that Spring. He had been a little concerned by my seeming to desert serious themes after I finished *The Four Winds of Love*. He was pleased to hear about my projected novel *Thin Ice* which I had finished that October. *Thin Ice* took as much out of me as any novel I have written. I was getting toward the end of it when I wrote to Faith just before the Edinburgh Festival:

I am in a state of agitated fury by the announcement that the Government is going to turn South Uist into a guided missile experimental range! This means death for the Outer Isles that were a refuge from this machine-ridden world of today.

A letter of protest in The Scotsman *has rallied a lot of people. Moray McLaren goes tomorrow to South Uist to attend a meeting of protest and to read a message from me. They have clearly sprung this on when Parliament wasn't sitting so that it would be a fait accompli by the time it meets again.*

I hope to get a public meeting here during the Festival. No sign of a buyer yet for Denchworth. I do wish it was off my hands.

I cannot tell you how this rocket business appals me.

No protests were of any avail against man's passion for those deadly toys. After threatening the old life of South Uist for the last fourteen years the rocketeers are now in 1969 threatening the lives of its lobsters.

On July 26 I wrote to Faith:

I'm up today after a fortnight of almost incessant pain. It has thrown back my work a great deal. I did get up about five days ago but was very bad next day. It's rather a nuisance.

Moray McLaren read what I've done of Thin Ice *and thinks it's very good.*

I shall get back to work on it tomorrow (D.V.) I'm glad that I've managed to get the television jobs put off till mid-September. I must finish this confounded book.

I shall have news of you when Lily comes back on Friday. I'm glad she has been so helpful for you.

I haven't energy to write a decent letter. The years rush and rush along.

After getting her diploma for beauty culture Lily came back to Drummond Place for a while and then decided to go through a course of hairdressing. She had been living with Faith in Sheffield Terrace for some time. Faith herself had gone to stay with Margaret Campbell on Canna. Chrissie went off with Jim and Alice Thomson for a holiday in Arran. I worked hard to get on with *Thin Ice* before we were overwhelmed in Drummond Place by the flood of Festival visitors. Somehow in spite of being rather exhausted first of all by Festival visitors and then by a lot of television I managed to reach the last chapter of *Thin Ice* before I went to Cheltenham for the Literary Festival. After Cheltenham I went to Bristol to gather material for *Sublime Tobacco*.

Income Tax was again becoming a problem because Denchworth

remained unsold, and it was unlikely that any purchaser would come along in the winter. However, in spite of financial anxiety Faith and I celebrated our golden wedding with a party at Wheeler's in Old Compton Street. In Octave 3 I told of our secret wedding and of our wedding breakfast at the Café Brice with my brother Frank. In those days lunch at the Café Brice cost two shillings in which wine and coffee were included.

The reason why we chose Wheeler's for that golden wedding party was that Wheeler's in 1905 was the Café Brice. We announced our wedding by sending cards for the New Year to all our friends. Now we sent the same card for the New Year of 1956. Here is the card with its accompanying jingle:

On November 30th 1905
Monty and Faith Compton Mackenzie
sent
A POSY OF SWEET MONTHS
to all their friends for 1906
from 7 Grosvenor Road, Westminster, SW
and Lady Ham, Burford, Oxon

On their Golden Wedding Day
they send the same Posy
to all their friends for 1956
from 31 Drummond Place, Edinburgh
and 13c Sheffield Terrace
Campden Hill, W8

A letter of mine to Faith with its allusion to the ridiculous shortage of winter water in Edinburgh sums up that party. It was written on December 11th:

Still laid up in bed! Railway travel is not my cup of tea. Can you remember if you sent Posies to the Linklaters? If not I will.

I thought everything went off splendidly. No news here except of dictating letters and reading books about tobacco. But, we've had some rain at last and I can pull the plug without a sense of guilt!

I hope you've recovered from all this excitement.

Both Flora Robson and my sister Fay were playing in Edinburgh that autumn. I had never met Flora Robson but within five minutes I felt I had known her for a long time. She made such an impression on me that I went to see her performance at the Lyceum. I recall

saying to the cloakroom attendant when I was handing in my hat
and coat that this was almost the only time that I had been to a
performance at the Lyceum since my first play was produced all but
fifty years ago.

"Then you ought to be ashamed of yourself, Sir Compton, and I
hope you'll be coming again next week when your sister will be
playing here."

I have to express apologetically that I cannot remember the
name of the play in which either actress performed. But though I
have forgotten the play I can remember being immensely impressed
by Flora Robson's performance.

Some time in this year 1955 I had a note from a Mr Roy Thomson
enclosing an introduction from Gladstone Murray who had been
the liaison between the B.B.C. and the Press and was later head, for a
time, of Canadian broadcasting. In this note of introduction I was
told that Mr Thomson had just bought *The Scotsman*.

When Roy Thomson arrived in Great Britain Lord Beaverbrook
had replied to a question about this fellow Canadian.

"He's a little man with a lot of little papers."

It was true that he did own a number of Canadian local
papers and at least one in Florida, but I recognised at once
that he was not a little man. What I liked about him was his complete candour when he told me he was not in the least interested in
politics or art when he was judging the value of a newspaper. All
he was interested in was its ability to earn money. I hear him
now as he leaves Drummond Place after his first visit: "Call me
Roy".

I shall not pretend that I foresaw the Fleet Street Empire that
Lord Thomson of Fleet would have built up in less than a decade,
but I was much taken by the complete absence of humbug or self-
deception. I was also much pleased by his appointment of Alastair
Dunnett as Editor of the new *Scotsman*.

On December 9th of this year he wrote me a letter which I hope
Lord Thomson will allow me to publish as he wrote it:

"Dear Monty,

You may have noticed in the newspapers recently that the
Independent Television Authority have now advertised for applica-
tions from those who desire to become the Programme Contractor
for the Independent Scottish Television Station.

"When we discussed this matter some time ago, you indicated

that you would be willing to become associated with us. It is necessary in our application to mention the names of those who have indicated their willingness to participate in our new Company, either as a shareholder or as a member of an Advisory Committee on programmes. I know you understand that I am not at all concerned about whether or not you invest any money in the Company. I am quite prepared to put up all of the capital necessary, but, of course, if those persons who become associated desire to take some of the stock, it will be available to them on exactly the same basis as my own.

"I am writing to you at this time to confirm that you have not changed your mind in connection with this matter, and that you will permit your name to be associated with us.

"Kind personal regards.

Yours sincerely,
Roy"

Alas, with the efforts I was making to stave off the demands of the Inland Revenue I did not feel that I was justified in investing more than the lowest amount of money required to become a shareholder. That was £33 10s. If, at that moment a purchaser had come along for Denchworth I might easily have invested a thousand pounds. Had I done so that investment would have been so justifiable that I should have been able to do no other work for two years than write the second volume of *Eastern Epic*. Enough about that failure which I still regret. If ifs were horses beggars would ride.

ABOUT the beginning of January the Edinburgh Income Tax Inspector was still refusing to accept my accountant's argument that the £649 which the move from Berkshire to Edinburgh had cost was an expense incurred in the pursuit of my profession.

While this argument was going on the *Daily Express* radio critic sneered at the B.B.C. for referring to Dennis Compton as Cumpton which they considered an affectation of which Dennis Compton himself disapproved. On top of this some clown wrote to a wireless paper to express surprise at my pronouncing the good old Scottish name of Compton as Cumpton and added that Dennis Compton had made a public protest against pronouncing his name with a 'u'.

I wrote to that wireless paper:

"Compton is not a 'good old Scottish name' as your contributor so rashly affirms. 'Compton' (always and everywhere pronounced 'Cumpton') is a frequent place-name in England from Devon to Northamptonshire occurring twenty-six times. It derives from the Welsh *cwm* (anglicised as *coomb* and *combe*) meaning a narrow valley in which is a *tun* or an enclosure. 'Compton' was presumably pronounced 'Coompton' and is often spelt as 'Cumptun' in medieval documents.

"If Mr Dennis Compton really did make a public protest against pronouncing his name 'Cumpton' he was displaying sad ignorance and putting himself out of step with the rest of the Cumpton company. The *Concise Oxford Dictionary* gives 18 words in which the prefix 'com' is pronounced 'cum'."

All through this Spring the argument about the expenses claimed by my accountant for the move from Denchworth to Edinburgh went on. I reprint one letter I wrote because I think that authors are still very hazy about this particular claim, and the fact that the Inland Revenue finally accepted my argument is a testimony to the reasonableness of the Inland Revenue and to my accountant's avoidance of anything that savoured of Clever Dickery or Smart Alecry.

"The point is that if the Inland Revenue wants me to go on earning money for them by writing books on which they are able to tax my publisher, my paper-maker, the booksellers, my printer, my binder, the circulating libraries and finally myself, they must recognise the necessity for me at the age of over 70 to decide where

I can write most fruitfully.   In my appeal[1] the Solicitor General
used a rubber grove in Malaya as a parallel case for my claim that
my transaction was capital not income. If I am in the same position
as a rubber grove and decide that it is necessary for me to replant
my trees, obviously that replanting would be allowed as an expense
connected with my earning capacity. The expense of moving from
the Channel Islands to Scotland was allowed in full, and though I
thought that the expense of moving from Barra to the South of
England had also been allowed I recognise that the generous allow-
ance made me for expenses during the time I was in the East was
to some extent the equivalent. Nevertheless, I think it would have
been more satisfactory to fight those moving expenses. I feel so
strongly that the full expense of my move to Edinburgh should be
allowed that I shall carry the question to the House of Lords if
necessary. I recognise that merely to move for the sake of moving
whenever he felt like it would have to be justified by the work such an
author produced in consequence. I am fortunately able to do that."

I do not recall the exact date, but it was while my accountant
was arguing with the Inland Revenue that the move from Berkshire
to Edinburgh should be allowed as a professional expense, the B.B.C.
were doing a series called *At Home* in the course of which the houses
of various people were visited by an interviewer with TV cameras.
My interviewer was Howell Davies whom I consider the best interviewer the B.B.C. have ever had. His death was a loss to broadcasting. I asked if when he came into my workroom he would look
round at the books and my writing chair and say:

"But this is a factory."

"Yes, that's just what it is and I hope some of the Inland Revenue
people are watching this programme."

During March of this year the Government seemed bent on
making a complete mess of the Cyprus situation and presently of
the whole of the Near East. The premature surrender of the Suez
Canal was to lead to the humiliating Suez fiasco later on this year.
How the Government managed to persuade itself that the develop-
ment of Cyprus as a basis of defence for the Near East would
compensate for the voluntary abandonment of Suez is incomprehen-
sible. That old British habit of hunting with the hounds and running
with the hare which had encouraged division between Hindus and

[1] In Octave 9 there is a full account of my Appeal against being charged
Income Tax on the sale of old copyrights.

Muslims, North and South Irishmen, Arabs and Israelis, was being repeated again in Cyprus between Greeks and Turks. Divide and rule served the Romans once upon a time but it was not a feasible policy for modern humanity. Various Labour Members recognised this, among whom Mrs Lena Jeger, the Member for South St Pancras, was the most active in her endeavour to instil simple common sense into the Government. Any chance of achieving an atmosphere of calm in Cyprus was destroyed by the Colonial Secretary's action in banishing Archbishop Makarios.

Letters to the Press at this date became more and more exasperating, and finally I was driven by a particularly irritating set of letters to *The Scotsman* to reply. In justice to the Editor he printed my very long letter:

"Your correspondents must try to get out of their heads the notion that the present state of affairs in Cyprus has anything to do with Communism. No Government in Europe has been more hostile to Communists than the Greek Government. There was a small Communist Party in Cyprus which today thanks to our handling of the situation is probably very much stronger than it was. A good chess-player knows how to take advantage of his opponent's bad moves.

"The inspiration of the Cyprus tragedy is a passionate longing to be united to Greece. In the middle of the last century the Ionian Islands had the same longing and in spite of Disraeli's attack upon the Government of the day for the threat to Turkey such a cession would mean and the help it would give the nefarious plans of Russia, statesmanship then prevailed.

"In 1878 Disraeli was given a lease of Cyprus, with the obligation to support Turkey against Russian aggression. The Cypriots liked the idea until they found that they would now have to pay taxes. The Turks, who had conquered Cyprus by massacring 20,000 of the inhabitants and flaying the Venetian Governor alive, had suppressed a revolt in 1764 with ferocity but since then they had left the Cypriots to their own devices.

"Under British administration the island remained stagnant for years. The Encyclopedia Britannica (1911) says: 'The Turks and British have added little and destroyed much, converting churches into mosques and grain stores.'

"In 1914 when Turkey, our loyal friend, went to war with us, we annexed the island. In 1915 we offered Cyprus to Greece if Greece would declare war on the Central Powers and go to the rescue of Serbia. If Venizelos had been still in power he might have taken the risk; as it was the offer was declined. After the 1914–18 war was over Venizelos was trying hard to make the Italians hand over Rhodes and therefore discouraged the Cypriot agitation for Union or *Enosis*. However, in Cyprus the struggle went on as it had gone on in Crete in 1909 when a British battalion supported by a Russian warship were discouraging the Cretans led by Venizelos from agitating for Union with Greece.

"In 1931 the resentment in Cyprus flared up and the Governor's residence was burnt. That Governor, the late Sir Ronald Storrs, a devoted friend of the island, told me he had always hoped to persuade the Colonial Office (Cyprus had by now been declared a Crown Colony) to take measures to win Cypriot esteem.

"After 1931 the desire for *Enosis* remained as fervid as ever, but there was not a single act of violence. It was only when one Conservative minister declared in the House that self-determination would never be granted and when another minister referred to the Greeks as an unreliable people that violence seemed to the Cypriots the only way of convincing the British Government that Cyprus did not want to be a British Colony.

"I ask your correspondents—the Colonels included—to cast their minds back to October 28, 1940. Britain stood alone. The world believed she was beaten. At 3 a.m. Mussolini presented an ultimatum to Greece which was rejected and Greece stood beside us. I am sure that even your correspondents cannot have forgotten what the Greeks did to that Italian offensive with all the help we could then afford, a few obsolescent planes most gallantly flown by the R.A.F. That sublime act of faith in herself and in Britain entitled Greece to a gratitude seldom owed by one country to another. Neither the raid on the Italian fleet in Taranto nor that superb advance of Wavell which led to Sidi Barani would have happened if Greece had yielded to Italy on that October night.

"In April 1941 we did our best to help Greece resist Hitler's rage but we failed, and Greece suffered a long agony under Nazi domination. During those years we helped the Greek resistance in the mountains, and as happened in so many other countries the toughest part of the resistance was provided by the communists. Even the historical ignorance that your correspondents all display is not so dense in the case of one of them but that he is able to remember what steps Sir Winston Churchill took in 1944 to deal with the situation in Greece after the liberation.

"If in 1945 we had voluntarily ceded Cyprus to Greece with the proviso that should the need arise we should be granted all the bases on the island we needed, Cyprus would be a happy island today. If, when after our surrender of the Suez Canal defences to Egypt and removal of our base to Cyprus we had given a solemn pledge of self-determination by a fixed date, violence could have been avoided, and the base secured. Our premature departure from Egypt has encouraged the Muslim revolt against French rule in North Africa, has encouraged the Arabs to believe they can overrun Israel, has made the Baghdad Pact a note of interrogation and has put fresh heart into the oil lobby in Washington. And to recover our prestige we preferred to subdue a small island of 400,000 hostile Greeks and 100,000 obsequious Turks.

"On whom lies the stigma, on Sinn Fein or the Black and Tans, of a Coalition Government? On William Wallace or Edward I?

"I have replied to your correspondents with deliberate moderation in the hope that people of historical and common sense without party prejudice will give themselves the trouble of reading this very long letter of mine."

Perhaps it was as well during those arguments I was having about Income Tax, Cyprus, the rocket range in South Uist, that I was writing a book about tobacco. Even reading and writing about tobacco had a mercifully sedative effect. Another sedative was a series of eleven readings I gave on radio of Graham Robertson's beautifully written book *Time Was*. It was gratifying to receive many letters from listeners because it showed that there were still plenty of people able to appreciate good prose. I take a gloomy view of the future of English prose but no doubt once upon a time gloomy views were taken of the future of Latin prose. I realised that when Ian Parsons wrote to tell me of an offer by Odhams to publish a condensed edition of *Ben Nevis Goes East*. I commented that these potted books were an unpleasant sign of the times, but that being a sign of the times one had to surrender to them.

I went down to London at the end of April to take the chair for a concert of the Gaelic Society of London and also to give a talk to the Inner Circle of the National Liberal Club. When I got back to Edinburgh I was rewarded for having done those two small jobs for music by meeting for the first time Yehudi Menuhin. He and his wife were good enough to pay us a visit in Drummond Place and I was deeply impressed by his wisdom. I had been lucky enough to hear every record he had made since his youthful years. He had now just had his fortieth birthday. I have forgotten what we talked about but the memory of the impression his conversation made upon me is still bright. Before they left Edinburgh Diana Menuhin was kind enough to send me a letter which made me feel that her husband knew that I had realised how wise he was:

I could not leave Edinburgh without thanking you for the lovely hour you allowed us to share with you this afternoon. You do not know what it means to two poor itinerants whose main conversations are based on Bradshaw and the Cunard sailings to be able to spend a civilised few moments with someone as rare and entertaining as yourself.

Yehudi is making a tremendous din at the moment on the scales necessary for Compleat Mastery of the violin—so please forgive this illiterate scrawl—it is hard to communicate with perforated ears. . . .

Yours with many thanks
Yehudiana Menuhin

That letter expressed perfectly what I was feeling about that hour with Yehudi and Diana Menuhin.

I had planned to write a book for Odhams which was to be called *The Bad Old Times* and was to consist of what seemed to me the most interesting cases in the Old Bailey Session Papers, the Annual Register, the Newgate Calendar and others from my large collection of criminal literature. In the end I had to cry off and a letter written at the end of the year explains why:

"I'm afraid I shall have to cry off *The Bad Old Days*. These eyes of mine are getting worse and worse and I must make use of them in a last effort to finish off my history of the Indian Army. My oculist will not operate yet for cataract and until this can be done intensive reading of old print is an impossibility. If by the end of next year I can get my eyes operated on and can feel I could definitely complete *The Bad Old Days* I shall let you know. I'm truly sorry to disappoint you like this but the tobacco book took me three times as long as I had reckoned on account of these eyes of mine, and I am fearful of going on with *The Bad Old Days* for the same reason."

Thin Ice was published in May and it was a joy to read a long review in the *Sunday Times* by Evelyn Waugh because he realised just how difficult a novel it had been to write. In *Vestal Fire* the comic side of homosexuality is stressed; in *Thin Ice* I should stress the tragic side. I read in a letter of congratulations on the wonderful Press *Thin Ice* had received but by now reviews favourable or unfavourable no longer interested me. To be sure when somebody like Evelyn

Waugh or Edmund Wilson praised a book of mine I was proud and humbly grateful but by the time the press-cuttings began coming in I was preoccupied with the next book I was writing and the last book was forgotten.

I have read the reviews of *My Life and Times* with attention but that is because *My Life and Times* is not yet finished and I cannot afford to forget the previous Octave any more than I could afford to forget the previous chapter when I was writing a novel.

Lily went to do her hairdressing course early that summer and was going to live with Jean and Arthur Howard at Emperor's Gate. Chrissie was amused to hear that her course began with Marcel waving. Indeed so was everybody else but apparently numbers of elderly ladies still went in for Marcel waving.

Faith came up to Scotland and after spending some time on Canna with Margaret Campbell came to stay in Drummond Place. Unluckily she slipped on stone stairs and was so badly shaken by her fall that I have always supposed that old age overtook her more rapidly after that fall. One would never suppose that she was in her seventy-ninth year. She could easily have passed for ten years younger than she was. She seemed to have recovered completely by the end of July and went back with Rosemary Russell to Sheffield Terrace, very anxious to get on with the book she was writing.

There return to me from that summer one or two delightful late nights after the play. One was when Cicely Courtneidge was playing in some musical comedy with her husband Jack Hulbert. It was very hard to believe that I had seen them first in *The Arcadians* over forty years ago. Her humour and verve at two o'clock in the morning were a marvel of vitality.

An even later night was spent in the enjoyment of Peter Ustinov's company. He was acting in his own play *Romanoff and Juliet* which I went to see and much enjoyed. However, I enjoyed much more Peter's gifts as a raconteur. He had the same ability as Ruth Draper to become in turn every person of whom he was talking, and his ability to reproduce the accent in English of a Scandinavian, a Frenchman, a German or indeed any nationality has never within my experience been equalled or even approached by any other raconteur. Moreover, he has a high intelligence and has laid down his knowledge of the world like a good wine. It was reassuring about contemporary students when he was recently elected Rector of Dundee University.

In May Roy Thomson had given a great banquet in the Assembly Rooms to meet General Alfred Gruenther, Supreme Allied Commander Europe. The hundred guests at that banquet were representative of Scottish administration, commerce, industry, medicine, law, literature and art.

Lord John Hope[1], then Joint Parliamentary Under-Secretary of State for Foreign Affairs, and Walter Elliot, the Lord High Commissioner Designate, gave the toast to the North Atlantic Treaty Organisation coupled with the name of General Alfred Gruenther, the guest of honour, who replied.

John Hope's wife Lisa was the daughter of Somerset Maugham. He would become Minister of Works two or three years later, and Edinburgh will remember him gratefully as the best Minister of Works Scotland has ever known. It was he who was responsible for clearing off the effects of reekie on the Royal Scottish Academy: indeed he was a Minister of good works.

I had a few minutes of talk with General Gruenther and recall being impressed by his cosmopolitan air.

That banquet in May was not such a huge affair as the Congress Banquet at the Savoy given by invitation of the English Centre to the International Pen Congress. I remember being told that there were 800 diners but that may have been an exaggeration.

Veronica Wedgwood[2] was President of the Congress, and she proposed P.E.N. replied to by Charles Morgan, President of International Pen. These speeches were followed by the toast of London by André Maurois to which I had to reply. I really did enjoy making that speech because it gave me an opportunity to say that the combined efforts of the Luftwaffe and our own in Air Defences during the last war had succeeded in doing only a fraction of the damage done to London by the London County Council, and with that I went on to mention some of their most vicious feats of vandalism like the destruction of Clifford's Inn and the ruining of Regent Street. The L.C.C. itself has now been destroyed; I wonder if the Greater London Council will equal the vandal record of their predecessors; I fear they will try their best.

The Queen Mother gave a garden party for the visitors at Clarence House. What I recall more vividly than any of the guests to whom I talked were the Bluebell matches which the footmen brought round with the cigarettes. I felt that the Queen Mother's love for Scotland was symbolised by those matches.

[1] 1st Baron Glendevon.   [2] Dame Veronica Wedgwood, O.M.

E

After that garden party I went on to dine with James and Helen Thurber at the Stafford Hotel by St James's Park. This, alas, was to be the last time I should see James Thurber. His theory that American writers and artists did not live so long as they did in Britain was sadly borne out.

I was relieved to find Faith seeming so much better when I went down to London that time. I was greatly cheered by at last getting rid of Denchworth Manor, although I had to let it go at a price ridiculously low. It was bought by Major Hague of Ovaltine. He was well liked in Denchworth and much missed when he was killed in a motor accident between Challow and Denchworth. A lot of alterations were made to bring the Manor into line with the stock-brokers' belt, but I was not at all sentimentally upset to hear of the changes. I had never fallen in love with Denchworth, even for a short while, and have never revisited it since I left in 1953.

As usual when one sells a house or property the purchasers are invited to bid for various articles. I find in a letter that Major Hague's solicitors had written to say their client was prepared to purchase the garden ladder, the garden roller, the billiard table, and the electric water heater, for which he suggested an all-in price of £60. I can never bring myself to haggle for more money with business men. I suppose it is a kind of superiority complex. I feel I shall cheapen myself if I haggle about money. The experience I had with Sir Percival Perry on Herm made me realise that one must be shameless if one is to be good at financial transactions.

In the autumn of this year I was able to attend the Wexford Festival. By now the Mayor and Corporation of Wexford had recognised that the Festival was something really important for Wexford, and all the streets were lighted with coloured lamps. What is more Dublin had realised that the Wexford Festival was a much more important achievement than Dublin had been willing to believe. Dublin made amends for its earlier scepticism by sending a special Opera Train on which the Dubliners would enjoy a good dinner before arriving.

In Wexford it was felt that this generous gesture by Dublin should be suitably acknowledged. So the Mayor and Corporation with the town band accompanied by various people responsible for the running of the Festival were waiting on the platform of Wexford railway station to receive the Dubliners. I forget what the tune was with which the town band welcomed the visitors but it was a loud enough noise to impress even Wagner.

I was pleased to meet for the first time Lord and Lady Harewood at a performance of Rossini's *La Cenerentola*. I hear now George Harewood turning to me in the first interval and saying with obvious astonishment,

"But this is really very good."

Although this was the first time I met Harewood he had corresponded with me as Editor of *The Gramophone* when he was still at Eton and what is more never wrote a letter about recordings of singers which had been made or were yet to be made that was not absolutely to the point. The fact that he expressed his obviously surprised approval of that performance of *La Cenerentola* was as great a compliment as Tom Walsh could ever receive.

It was in October of this year that Randolph Churchill won a case he had brought against some newspaper and I had telegraphed my congratulations when he wrote:

"I had the good fortune to meet you in the interval between receiving your telegram and having the opportunity to answer it. I write to thank you, none the less, and to say that none of the kind messages I have received has given me greater pleasure than yours.

Yours ever

Randolph"

Randolph Churchill had a reputation for rudeness but whenever I have heard him being rude I was well able to understand why he was rude. It is a tragic loss to history that he did not live to finish the life of his father which started with that fascinating first volume. His son Winston handled his adversaries in the TV discussion about that pretentious German play which set out to suggest that Winston Churchill had planned the death of General Sikorski in the plane crash at Gibraltar. I have never been able to understand how such a wretched piece of fiction was produced in an English theatre. In spite of young Winston's admirable performance I could not help regretting that Randolph was not there to obliterate Kenneth Tynan and one or two others.

There was anxiety that November in 1956 about Winston Churchill's health and I was asked by the B.B.C. Overseas Service to write and record a half-hour obituary for *London Calling Asia*. When I finished what I had written I showed the script to Bob Boothby to be reassured and I was much relieved when Bob gave it the 'all clear'.

My happy association with Grants as a witness to the merits of

Standfast whisky had been active for some months when at the end of October I received a letter from Eric Roberts, the Joint Managing Director:

"I have learned with much pleasure that you are valiantly making the hurried trip to London and back on November 14th so that you can be present at the Press Conference in the Savoy over the new bottle.

"Mather and Crowther have booked for yourself and me on 'The Chieftain' which takes off from Turnhouse at 8 a.m. We have to report 20 minutes before that hour so I shall call for you on the 14th at 7 a.m.

"Our return by the afternoon plane has also been fixed."

Eric Roberts and I reached Turnhouse in good time and the plane rose into the air punctually. All went well until we ran into fog and the plane having been warned off Heathrow for the present went round and round above Watford for nearly two hours. With that great boon of old age, immunity from sea-sickness, neither was I airsick but nearly everyone else in the plane was.

We reached the Savoy just before lunch. By the time I had toasted the admirable shape of the new bottle at that lunch it was time for Eric Roberts and me to set off again for Heathrow. That new bottle has been presiding over Piccadilly Circus ever since. It was a particularly jolly gathering at the Savoy and I wished that I did not have a speaking engagement that evening in Edinburgh which took me away from it too soon.

Eric Roberts wrote:

"I hope that I managed to convey to you our very grateful thanks for the effort you made despite your other and prime commitments to come to the function in London.

"We would like to mark the introduction of the new bottle by giving you something which you would like to have, and as you mentioned to me that you did not have a television set I would be glad to know whether the gift of a television set would be acceptable to you."

That H.M.V. television set has been giving us pleasure in Drummond Place for twelve years.

Those words were written in October 1969 just before I had to stop work on this Tenth Octave until I could get more powerful glasses.

On hearing about this trouble with my eyes Eric Roberts made my Christmas memorable by giving me a colour television. I take this opportunity of stressing the value of colour television for failing eyesight.

Here is a letter from Eric Roberts about the début of the triangular bottle:

"January 8. 1970.

Dear Monty,

"That was the occasion when we were introducing the triangular bottle at the Savoy Hotel. I remember the designer, Hans Schleger, in his speech saying that a triangular bottle had been the dream of glass manufacturers 'since the days of Rome'. Not long afterwards I found myself in Australia and in hot water with the Pharmacy Boards of all the States when I proposed to introduce the triangular bottle there. It seemed that about fifty years ago all the brewers had tried to stop the practice of the farmers up-country returning their empty beer bottles, a percentage of which had been used to hold kerosene, with consequential adverse effect on the flavour of the beer when the bottles were refilled. Their solution to this problem was to require all these obnoxious liquids and dangerous things, like phenol, to be sold only in triangular bottles! I am glad to say that so far as I know nobody yet has ever drunk a slug of kerosene in mistake for Standfast."

The wretched mess up of the Suez business hung heavily over us. First of all the premature withdrawal from Egypt and the stupid belief that Cyprus would be as useful a base for the Levant, and then the badly planned British–French–Israeli attack.

It would be Harold Nicolson's[1] birthday on November 21st and 255 guests had subscribed £1370 as a present which would enable him and Vita Sackville-West to go on that cruise to Java the story of which he preserved in a book.

I find a note to me:

"Sissinghurst Castle,
Cranbrook, Kent.
November 26, 1956.

My dear Monty,

"How very good of you to contribute to the sumptuous gift presented to me on my seventieth birthday. We hope to go off on the proceeds for a winter cruise, a luxury we could never have contemplated had it not been for the generosity of our friends.

[1] The late Sir Harold Nicolson, K.C.V.O.

"My word what a mess we are in! I know we ought not to stab the Prime Minister in the back but I have a feeling he should not have shown it so readily.

Yours ever,
Harold"

In my reading during old age the books I have most enjoyed are the three volumes of Harold Nicolson's *Diaries and Letters*. I find in the third volume an entry in his diary of 15th November, 1951:

"In the evening I take the chair at a B.B.C. Forum on the theme 'Are cliques necessary?' I had Bob Boothby and Kingsley Martin and we have a good discussion. I speak about the Souls, Kingsley about Bloomsbury and Bob about Cliveden and Sibyl (Colefax). We say that the disappearance of Society means that young men have no opportunity of meeting the great men of our age."

I doubt if Harold Nicolson in his most pessimistic mood in 1951 could have imagined the calamitous vulgarisation effected by the sexy 'sixties.

That mention of Sibyl Colefax takes me back to so many evenings in what had become Lord North Street since I lived there. I recall a dinner engagement in September 1950 and being rung up at the Savile by Sibyl's maid to say that her Ladyship was terribly disappointed that she would not be well enough for her dinner party and so it would have to be put off. She died next morning. It used to be said that when you were asked to tea by Lady Colefax you had your foot on the first rung of the ladder, that when you were asked to lunch you were quite a way up and that when you were asked to dinner you had securely arrived at the top of it. Those who were not given the freedom of Sibyl Colefax's salon used to laugh at her anxiety to back winners, and I remember the crude amusement caused by an advertisement in the agony column of *The Times* to say that Lady Colefax had lost her engagement book and begging anybody who found it to return it to her.

Those who have read Harold Nicolson's *Diaries* will know what evenings those were at 19 Lord North Street. After Emerald Cunard died the only ones which competed with them and mercifully are still to be enjoyed were the dinner-parties of Yvonne and Jamie Hamilton.

In his diary for 28th April 1952 Harold Nicolson wrote:

"I have a B.B.C. discussion with Monty Mackenzie on getting old. He contends that there is no difference at all. I contend that it is the greatest of human tragedies. He contends that physically there are few disadvantages. What does it really matter if one walks two miles an hour instead of four miles an hour? He notices no difference in his memory, character or powers of invention. It was a good discussion."

I was then going to be 70 in nine months time. Harold was all but a couple of months four years younger. I find now at 87 that I forget people's names occasionally and more regrettably owing to my wretched eyesight people's faces, but mercifully my power to concentrate on work in hand has not in the least diminished.

I always thought that Harold Nicolson's handicap was his shyness. If he met one of his friends for the first time after a lapse of time he would cover his shyness by saying what anybody who did not know him well would have supposed to be something deliberately rude. After he joined the Savile he asked me on one of my rarer appearances why all the younger members of the Club avoided him. I explained that it was the custom for junior members to talk to their seniors without waiting for any formal introduction.

"Exactly," said Harold Nicolson, "that was what I was looking forward to when I joined."

"Well, I'm afraid you frighten them, Harold."

"Frighten them?" he repeated in obvious astonishment.

I have also thought that one of the reasons why Harold Nicolson was such a superlative broadcaster was the enjoyment he had from being in company alone. Nevertheless, when he was really deeply moved as he was by the folly of appeasement he made at least one great speech in Parliament. Lord Randolph Churchill once admitted near the end of his disappointed life that in his heart he was a Liberal. I feel that Harold Nicolson in spite of being a member of the Labour Party was at heart a Conservative. I think if Harold Nicolson and I were to debate old age together in a broadcast today we should both agree that the tragedy of age is the loss of dear friends younger than oneself: for me one of those friends was Harold Nicolson. In the third volume of his *Diaries* I read his entries about Cyprus at this date and it is always a joy to read the opinions of other people with which one is in accord.

I was invited by the Greek Government to pay a three weeks visit to Greece and travel all over the country. Unfortunately I was so tied up with engagements that I had to refuse what would have been a splendid holiday to celebrate the completion of *Sublime Tobacco*. One of these engagements was a farewell dinner given by the Croquet Association to the very successful New Zealand test team. As President I was in the Chair and had the pleasure of toasting those warm-hearted New Zealanders whose visit was as much a tonic for British Croquet as fifty years earlier the All Blacks had been for Rugby football.

Another promise to keep that autumn was to be called as a witness for the defence in an action being brought against Antonia White for libel. I first met Antonia White at 22 Penham Road, West Kensington, when she was an infant in arms called Eirene Botting. I have written of her father C. G. Botting in my Second Octave; he was a good friend of my boyhood. He became a Catholic and Antonia White was sent to a fashionable convent school at Roehampton. Of this school she wrote a moving story called *Frost in May* which had a well deserved success. I cannot recall what was the libel complained of and I did not know any of the plaintiffs but I was called to witness to the defendant's integrity. I never enter a law court without thanking God I had enough sense to give up any notion of making the Bar my profession.

On December 5th I wrote to Faith:

Fay (without knowing it) is to be 'This is Your Life' on TV on December 10 at 7.15. I've asked her to meet me at 13C. Sheffield Terrace at 5.30. I'll be along before she arrives. It's a nuisance having to come down to London but I didn't like to deprive her of the opportunity and they wouldn't do it unless I agreed to come down.

I have to deal with the Winston obituary for East and Far East at 200 Oxford Street and I must get back that night because I have to do another broadcast here next day. Phew!

Oh, dear what a mess we are in in the Near East, the Middle East as they will call it. I'd make every newly appointed Cabinet Minister pass an examination in geography before the door was opened to let him in.

On American Television the programme *This is Your Life* had been a great success and it was now being copied in Great Britain but less ruthlessly and in a more gentlemanly way. There subjects were often confronted with some scandal in the past. The B.B.C. never did this: it had not forgotten all the lessons that Lord Reith had taught it. It is a relief to learn that the Press Council had censured the *News of the World* for pandering to the promiscuity which affects the public at the end of the sexy 'sixties.

Little did I know when I wrote that letter to Faith that on November 19th Leslie Jackson, the producer of *This is Your Life*, had written to her from the Television Studios at Shepherd's Bush:

"Dear Lady Mackenzie,

As producer of the television programme 'This is Your Life' we have for some time been attempting to present the life story of Sir Compton as a long overdue tribute to him. We plan that this broadcast should come as a surprise to him, and we hope to produce it, should you be good enough to approve of the idea, on December 10th.

"I should very much like to come and talk the matter over with you some day next week, and Mr Christopher Stone, who is helping us in this venture, will be telephoning you to explain the nature of the programme.

"It is, of course, vital that Sir Compton does not hear of our intentions, and I would ask you to keep the matter entirely secret from him. This, I fear, sounds very mysterious, but I hope that Christopher Stone will explain everything to your satisfaction.

Yours sincerely,
T. Leslie Jackson"

Nor did I know that Peter Moore of *This is Your Life* team had written to Chrissie:

"Dear Miss MacSween,

As Sir Compton has as I expect told you, I shall be travelling up to Edinburgh on Thursday, to keep an appointment with him at 4 o'clock. No doubt he will also have told you that he intends to travel up to London on December 9th to take part in a television programme on the evening of the 10th, so I am writing to explain to you our plans.

"With the backing of Lady Mackenzie, Christopher Stone, Mrs Viola Crocker, Mr Martin Secker and others, we are hoping to present Sir Compton as the subject of a 'This is Your Life' programme on December 10th. At the suggestion of Fay Compton we have adopted the simple subterfuge of inviting Sir Compton to participate in a similar programme with her as the principal subject, in whose life story he would naturally take part. When I see Sir Compton on Thursday, I shall do my best to maintain this subterfuge, (despite, no doubt, a searching inquisition) but in addition, I am most anxious to talk to you, who have also played an integral part in his life story.

"I hope to fly up during the morning, and wonder whether it

would be possible for you to have lunch with me, or for me to see you during the afternoon, other than at 31 Drummond Place, because, of course, Sir Compton must not know that I am also interviewing you, and hoping to persuade you to appear in the programme about his life.

"Yesterday, I saw Kenny McCormick and Mr John Hope-Johnston, who will also be appearing, so I am sure you will agree that already we have a number of pleasant surprises for Sir Compton.

"I shall be most grateful if you will let me know whether we may meet on Thursday before 4 o'clock. As a confidential secretary this must, I am afraid, trouble your conscience, but I am certain of persuading you of the worthiness of the cause!

Yours sincerely,

Peter Moore"

And I am amused to read now the letter that Chrissie wrote to Faith on November 27th:

"Peter Moore is coming up here on Thursday about this pro-gramme—not telling him of course that it is a surprise for himself—but working on the assumption that it is all for Fay. He has written to me telling me of those taking part and says I must do so also. C.M. has actually just said to me 'I hope they are not going to spring anything on me by pretending it is for Fay!' to which I've replied 'Oh no! I don't think so for surely they would have asked me too.' So I shall have to go on pretending not to know much about it which isn't ever easy with him as you so well know. Peter Moore is going to have a hard task—he doesn't begin to know what he is up against. But that is their funeral. So I expect I shall see you next Monday week—I had no intention of coming to town at all for a very long time. There seems such a lot to do and we are getting on well with all sorts of jobs—book cataloguing, press cuttings, etc., etc. I am glad that Lily will soon be coming up."

I was concentrated on the Winston Churchill obituary for the East and Far East which I was going to record on the day after the 'This is Your Life' programme. Peter Moore had arranged with Chrissie that she was to come down to London by the night train and I upset all the arrangements by refusing to go down to London in the morning.

"You know perfectly well," I said to Chrissie, "that I never travel by day if I can help it. You'd better ring the Savile at once and tell them to cancel my room. I don't know why you booked it for the night of the 9th. I will be there on the night of this confounded business and I shall come back on the night of the 11th."

When I got to the Savile I found a note from Faith to ask me not to come to Sheffield Terrace but to meet Fay at the flat in Emperor's Gate where Lily was living with Jean and Arthur Howard. Supposing as I did that Fay was to be the subject of the programme I went on wondering why the B.B.C. wanted her and me to go to the King's Theatre, Hammersmith, and then presumed it was because it was going to be Christopher Stone's life.

"And where's Jean?" I asked.

"She's with Faith," I was told.

When a car called to take me to Hammersmith I expected that Fay was coming with me and was surprised when Arthur Howard told me that he would be driving Fay and Lily to the theatre. I shook my head over the muddled way in which everybody was behaving and went off in the car sent for me.

Just before we reached the King's Theatre the chauffeur turned off to the right. I asked him where he was going to which he replied "The King's Theatre".

"But you're going in the wrong direction," I protested.

"No, sir, it's round here."

"I know every inch of the road between Hammersmith Broadway and Addison Bridge. I could find my way blindfold to the King's Theatre. You evidently suppose we're going to the TV studios in Lime Grove."

With splendid tact the chauffeur, realising that I knew where the King's Theatre was, said quickly.

"What was I thinking of, sir? I had got into my head we were going to Lime Grove."

Whereupon he turned and we arrived at the stage door of the King's Theatre where I was taken up to a dressing room. There I was told Eamonn Andrews would be along very soon.

"I hope he will," I said, "I want to go through my bit about Fay before the show starts."

Eamonn did not arrive and I began to grumble in spite of an assurance that he would soon be with me.

"Extraordinary lot of amateurs you still are at the B.B.C.," I grumbled. "You're as amateurish as a film studio."

At last Eamonn Andrews arrived and I reproached him for giving his instructions so late.

"Now, what is the first question you are going to ask me about

Fay?" I said as I took my seat in the chair to which he pointed. The curtain went up and Eamonn was saying, "This is Your Life."

I was taken aback for a brief moment, but having been taunting the amateurishness of the B.B.C. I had to behave professionally and I was immediately at ease. One after another of the 'Cast' came in— Faith, Viola, Fay, Jean, Christopher, Hope-Johnston and, to my astonishment, Chrissie whom I had left behind in Edinburgh the night before. She had been flown down next morning.

To my pleasure Faith had a great success. I have beside me as I write of that December evening thirteen years ago the notes scribbled by Faith for her piece with Eamonn Andrews:

Yes. At Oxford when he was an undergraduate and a very alarming young man he was.

But you married him none the less? Despite parental opposition?

No, they had no chance of opposition. How could they? we were secretly married in church.

He had a passion for living on islands?

A passion which I shared and would again. But it has meant that in all those years we have never lived for more than seven years in one home. We lived in Capri before it became the Isle of Capree and lost its character. Then the Channel Islands, Herm the haunted and its beloved little neighbour Jethou, and then Barra in the Hebrides. Wonderful!

Happily married to a human earthquake? How have you managed it?

Well, perhaps I might quote from a poem I like very much which goes:

"Give your hearts but not into each other's keeping,
And stand together, yet not too close together,
For the pillars of the temple stand apart
And the oak and the cypress do not grow in each other's shade."

That's all but I might put it more simply. Love and let live. Is that enough?

Faith had a heavy mail from viewers, many of whom asked where they could find the words she had quoted. They come from *The Prophet* by Kahlil Gibran published by Heinemann. I have not read the book myself.

Faith had such a success with her part in *This is Your Life* that the B.B.C. asked her to repeat her extract in another programme they were doing. I have never heard of any other extract from *This is Your Life* being given an encore.

I have been in the lives of three or four other people since then not to mention various others of Eamonn Andrews' programmes, and I record now my admiration for his unique gift for putting people at their ease under the lights of television, and also my affection for him.

Just before Christmas I received a letter which seemed to have been brought by Santa Claus himself:

I became an admirer of your writing at the age of 4 and I have never ceased to read your books since. Your Santa Claus in Summer was the first love of my childhood and has seen me through many years since until I foolishly lent it to some children who lost it for me.

Now that I have a four year daughter myself I feel she will be missing something without your wonderful book. I would be so grateful if you could give me some idea where or how I could obtain a copy as it has been out of print for ages.

By the same welcome post came a New Year's card from Rose Macaulay whose fascinating novel *The Towers of Trebizond* I had been able to salute in the *News Chronicle*:

"DEAR MONTY how kind and generous you are! That you should like my TOWERS and say so is so delightful to me. It has been sustained all along by a remark of yours which Collins used—and now you praise it in the NEWS CHRONICLE.

"My love and thanks, dear veteran contemporary, and may 1957 bring from you a book as good as *Thin Ice*.

Rose"

"Dear Rose Macaulay,

I see you now in a flutter from getting back to the B.B.C. for a broadcast after you had been given an Honorary D.Litt. from Cambridge. You were still wearing the dress for the ceremony and I exclaimed, "Rose! you look like a Light Blue Hungarian Hussar! It's lucky for you that the B.B.C. Home Guard is a thing of the past. They would never have let you in while the war was on.""

I STARTED the year by getting down to a novel I was proposing to call *Deuce* but the title of which I changed to *Mezzotint*. On January 16th I wrote to Faith:

I've been wrestling with the first 20 pages of 'Deuce' and have finished them at last. The beginning of a novel is always hell.

Five days later I wrote:

"Forgive dictating but my leg is jumping a great deal. The usual result of starting a new book. . . . I've had to put 'Deuce' aside to correct the galleys of 'Sublime Tobacco': and I am indeed a galley-slave this time. . . .

"I have been asked to go to China in April for 6 weeks, but I have said 'no'. I think it would be too tiring and there will be too many factories to be shown over. Rose Macaulay is going!"

Gladys Cooper came to Edinburgh that January with an American musical. Chrissie wrote to Faith on January 29:

"A ghastly show (which I have not seen but heard about from others) is here this week with Gladys Cooper called The Crystal Heart, an American Musical. They were booed on the first night, which hardly ever happens in Edinburgh, and the notices in today's papers made one feel so sorry for the wretched actors.

"Gladys Cooper is now off ill and not to appear for the rest of the week. She had to be given sedatives etc., after the first night, which is not surprising. Everything that could go wrong apparently went wrong, and when the understudy came on for the matinee yesterday she had to read the script because there hadn't been time for her to study, and I hear she did the same in the evening. It sounds a dreadful fiasco."

No wonder I was feeling more and more pessimistic about the contemporary stage.

After struggling for a while with *Deuce* I had given it up and started instead to write *Rockets Galore*. Then in the middle of February I was rung up by the B.B.C. to ask if I could possibly go to Nice in two days time to interview Somerset Maugham and Robert Service for the television series A to Z. M was due very soon and Alan Melville who was to have interviewed Maugham had lost a relative and could not go.

"It means I'll have to come down to London tomorrow morning," I hesitated.

I was thinking about my infernal leg.

"Oh, all right," I said at last, "I'll go."

A sigh of relief from the B.B.C. was audible.

On Valentine Day Chrissie wrote to Faith:

"C.M. has agreed to fly to the South of France tomorrow to do a TV interview with Somerset Maugham. . . . He is quite excited about the trip and I think it will be nice for him. He goes down to London by the last train tomorrow and will drive from King's Cross straight to Heathrow.

"I must dash out now with his passport which has to be posted to them in London to deal with it for currency etc., etc.

"Last weekend a severe attack and this weekend this! What a man!"

My pleasant companion on this trip was Bryan Sears, the extremely competent producer. When I got into the plane at Heathrow I saw Winston Churchill already seated. I asked Lady Churchill if I might salute the great man. She shook her head and said, "He does not recognise people easily."

Nowadays I too find it less easy to recognise people.

There was a note from Willie Maugham at the hotel in Nice inviting me and my companion to dinner that night at the Villa Mauresque.

Cocktails at 7.45: Dinner at 8.
I am so looking forward to seeing you.

Yours always
W.S.

Of course day clothes!!!

I felt that Maugham really was glad to see me and he asked almost affectionately after Faith.

Maugham was now 83 and I was much impressed by the tact with which Alan Searle, his secretary, handled him. I recall a rather grumpy demand to know if Alan had remembered to let the dogs out. The dogs were two Pekinese with one of whom I had a success. I imitated the noise Pekes made when breathing and he jumped up on my knee. Maugham was obviously astonished:

"I've never known him to do that to anybody," he said.

"He obviously thought I was another Peke, Willie."

It was a most agreeable evening, from which the only snatch of conversation I recall was my observing to Maugham what long lobes he had to his ears and that long lobes were considered in the Highlands a sign of longevity.

When we got back to the Villa Mauresque on Sunday morning Maugham decided it was too blowy for any outdoor work and said that he would like the talk with me to take place in the study at the top of the tower. The camera-men had had an uncomfortable and tiring night in a Dakota with their heavy equipment and nowhere to sit except the floor. However, they were quite cheerful about the job of carrying all their heavy paraphernalia to the top of the tower and the interview started at half-past ten.

It was a tricky business because from time to time Maugham was in a stammering paroxysm and I would sit motionless until it had subsided. I knew that when the stammering was cut out it would be necessary for me to look exactly as I was looking when the paroxysm began. For me those paroxysms gave a new comprehension of William Somerset Maugham. Until that February morning I had never heard more than a hesitant repeat of the opening consonant, and I had always thought that Maugham had exaggerated the effect of a stammer in youth and made it as in *Of Human Bondage* as much of an infliction as a club foot. I realised now how his hatred of school had been those paroxysms of once upon a time which his school fellows mocked.

It was close on half-past one when the interview came to an end. "If you care to take p-pot luck," Maugham said to Bryan Sears and myself, "you can stay to lunch."

Then Alan Searle whispered something to Maugham.

"No, no," Maugham said, "they can get back to their hotel."

Obviously Alan Searle had suggested offering the camera team lunch. He murmured something again.

"No, no, they'll be getting back to their hotel," Maugham repeated irritably.

I do not think the refusal of drinks to the camera team was due to Maugham's notorious closeness over money. I think after what for him was a long ordeal he wanted to forget all about television and enjoy the pot luck of his lunch. Nevertheless, there is no doubt that Maugham's last years were haunted by money. Those deplorable autobiographical memoirs published by the *Sunday Express* and in book form in America, though not in Britain, were written because he could not bring himself to refuse the large sum of money with which Beaverbrook tempted him.

The contrast between the atmosphere of the Villa Mauresque of Cap Ferrat and the Villa Aurore of Monte Carlo when we went next day for the interview with Robert Service was as sharp as the contrast between the two men who owned them. The Villa Mauresque had been the nest of a lovebird of King Leopold of Belgium: the Villa Aurore had been a brothel.

"I bought it cheap over thirty years ago and got a good price for the nine bidets."

In this February Maugham and Service were both a month over 83: I was a month over 74. Service had white hair, rosy cheeks and a loud voice: Maugham was now beginning to shrivel.

Service had been a junior bank clerk in Glasgow. When he emigrated to Canada he became a bank clerk again and was sent to Dawson City in Yukon, with all the excitement of the Klondyke gold rush. His *Songs of a Sourdough* had been a great success when they were first published and were still selling. His facility for writing what he called pieces (he would not call them poems) was almost alarming. He told me his ambition was to write a thousand pieces before he died "And my hobby is longevity", he added with a roar of laughter.

The room in which we were discussing the interview looked out over the bay, and it was suggested for the camera's benefit that we should sit out on the overhanging balcony. It was in full sunshine but there was a cold wind blowing and after a while I began to feel as if Service and I actually were in the Alaska of which we were talking. I was glad when we got indoors again and Service summoned the camera crew to drink a toast to the interview in champagne. That was another sharp contrast to yesterday in the Villa Mauresque. I was sad to hear about eighteen months later that Service had failed to reach the extra-old age for which he hoped.

I enjoyed that brief visit to the Riviera but as I wrote to Faith, "I have no desire to retire to the French Riviera. Nothing but cars and building going on all the time everywhere."

As a result of sitting out on that Mediterranean balcony in Alaska I had a few days in bed when I got back to Drummond Place and did not get to work again on *Rockets Galore*. Chatto's would be able to publish in the autumn if I could finish it by April. I had written regretfully to Magdalen Eldon[1] to say that I might not be able to finish *Deuce* with which I was wrestling. I felt more optimistic over *Rockets Galore* and a letter from Magdalen made me absolutely

[1] The late Countess of Eldon.

F

determined to lay that Easter Egg as a reward for industry in the Victorian fashion.

I had just been rereading that letter of February 1957 when the news of Magdalen's death reached me in France. Here is my brief tribute to her in *The Times* of October 13, 1969:

"May one who had known Magdalen Eldon for nearly forty years pay this small tribute to her artistry, humour, kindness and beauty? Of that artistry I was a grateful debtor when at the age of 17 she illustrated my novel *Our Street* in perfect sympathy with the characters she depicted and with the period in which they lived. Her kindness was insatiable and the recipients of it were encouraged to suppose that she was grateful to them for giving her an opportunity to be kind. Her humour was constant and what more enchanting qualities may any woman be granted than humour and beauty? Of that beauty she never seemed in the slightest bit aware, and through all the years of my long life I have met barely half a dozen women as beautiful as she was."

And here are a few words from that letter I had just been reading when I heard she had left us:

Darling Monty,

How lovely that you really and truly can come for Easter. It should be so lovely down here by then—altho' the daffodils are already practically over now and the roses and the peonies poking through. It is the wildest wettest Spring—not a frost in sight (just started a snow-shower!). So all the delphiniums will most likely greet you instead.

Everyone is shaking their heads and saying it spells disaster but so far it only spells crocuses and snowdrops and lots of very wet lambs. . . .

I hope to have the boys and Hugh and A.[1] Your train from London to Taunton 2½ hours only. Come to us in Holy Week, at least make it a long weekend.

Your very very loving
Magdalen

I was already wondering what I should do after I finished *Rockets Galore* and *Mezzotint* and wrote to Gerald Beadle to suggest a possible TV programme for next year:

"Dear Gerald,

I have just come back from an extremely pleasant trip to the Riviera where I interviewed W. S. Maugham and Robert Service

[1] Lady Antonia Fraser.

for the A to Z series. Bryan Sears was with me as producer and of course a camera team. I was so immensely struck by the skill and good humour with which everything was handled that I was seized with an ambition to undertake a much more elaborate adventure with the same five people.

"I am wondering whether TV would consider an expedition to Greece to do a series:

1. Mythological stories (Iliad, Odyssey, Argonauts etc.) for schools.
2. Historical stories (Marathon, Salamis, etc., etc.) for schools.
3. A series of all the famous sites—Delphi, Knossos, Olympia, Mycenae, Sparta, Parnassus etc., etc. for adult viewers, and possibly
4. A series of tales of War 1 from Gallipoli to Rhodes against the background of the actual adventure.

"I would do the writing and the talking against the appropriate background, and it ought to be possible to get a good many hours of varied television entertainment and instruction.

"If the experiment proved a success one could do Italy on the same lines.

"I am 'well seen' by the Greeks, and I am sure we could get the maximum help from the authorities. The ideal months for the Aegean are October and April. I don't think I could manage October of this year, but April and May of next year would be all right for me.

"This letter is not meant as it were officially but is personal to yourself and if you think the scheme a madcap notion tell me so as you would tell me in conversation at the Savile.

"I do believe that the possibilities of this experiment are considerable, but if I am to help in making it it mustn't be delayed too long: I shall be 75 next January."

I had forgotten that the idea for the TV programme *The Glory that was Greece* came from me. If I had not found that letter I should have given the B.B.C. all the credit for it. I ought not to have forgotten Gerald Beadle's generously encouraging reply to that letter of mine. On March 1st he wrote from Television Centre, Wood Lane:

"Dear Monty,

Your letter is a most interesting one and, if I may say so, typical of your genius and vitality.

"I think the best thing to do would be for you to get together with Kenneth Adam, who has recently been appointed Controller Television Programmes. He knows about your suggestions and would be delighted to meet you and discuss this project. Will you make direct contact with him?

Yours ever,
Gerald Beadle."

I wrote to Kenneth Adam to say that I expected to be in London toward the end of the month and that if he thought there was anything worth considering in my suggestion about Greece I should be available to discuss it. He wrote back to make a lunch date at Television Centre for March 24.

I took Wilfred Taylor of *Scotsman's Log* to the Nomads Dinner that March. As I record that fact I am happy to think that the *Scotsman's Log* in *The Scotsman* is still rolling along as indomitably as ever. I think I can salute *Scotsman's Log* as the best example of a journalistic marathon since G. R. Sims was writing *Mustard and Cress* every week for the *Reference* from 1877 until 'Dagonet' died in 1922. I shall not be alive to congratulate Wilfred Taylor on equalling that feat of G. R. Sims but if when I depart he is still writing *Scotsman's Log* I know that he will write as kindly about me as he has written of so many mutual friends who have gone before.

Chatto and Windus have recently (1969) republished that remarkable novel *In Accordance with the Evidence* by Oliver Onions. Like myself Moray McLaren could never understand why English literary critics had not realised what a fine writer Oliver Onions was. Moray McLaren had written an article about King's Cross in *The Scotsman* in which he alluded to *In Accordance with the Evidence*. Oliver Onions wrote to him, and Moray McLaren gave me this letter which I have fortunately found. I wrote a word or two about Oliver Onions in Octave Nine when telling about the 70th birthday lunch at the Garrick Club for Martin Secker. Here is the letter to Moray McLaren:

"Dear Mr McLaren,

I think it was your use of the word 'topicality' that startled me the most. I am referring of course to your King's Cross article in the 'Scotsman' of February 28th. Little did I ever think to hear that old string vibrate again anyway, but that 'In Accordance with the Evidence' should be still alive and kicking, however feebly! The only conclusion is that in Edinburgh anything can happen.

"But it can happen too late, and as time has gone on I have understood these things less and less. In fact if I now had the arranging of my own 84th birthday party I should hardly know who to ask. The last reunion of the sort I was at was Secker's own 70th, but as far as I remember the only two of the Original Contemptibles present were Monty Mackenzie and myself. Actually I have made very few friends among writers. In 1900 when my first book was published, I had already served two apprenticeships, and my associates were mostly painters, sculptors and commercial artists. I cannot think who sets these legends going, that I learnt my writing in French on the Left Bank (which I never did), was a fellow-roisterer of Dylan Thomas's (whom I never set eyes on and who was forty years my junior anyway), that the only reason why I did not swing for 'In Accordance' was that the police couldn't find the body, and so on. Anybody would think that I'd been turning away from publishers and publication instead of hammering at every door I came to since 1900!

"In short, for the shabby pass writing is in today anybody's guess is as good as mine. Publishers, authors, the trade, we've all had a finger in it more or less, and the book I am trying to get through now will quite definitely be my last. But it is now a struggle back to convalescence in addition to the years, and my wife now in her 78th year, has her hands more than full. I have had one or two copies made of what you say about 'In Accordance'. One can only try, but it makes all the difference to find one has more friends in the world than one knew of. If anything comes of it, a belated 'Penguin' say, I will let you know. I should hate to let those down in the end who have been faithful to me for so long.

Yours sincerely,
Oliver Onions."

I was much encouraged by that lunch at Television Centre and thought it a good omen that it took place on the eve of Greek Independence Day. It was my first meeting with Kenneth Adam but Grace Wyndham Goldie had once or twice been a particularly helpful producer of talks I had done with her in pre-Television days. Grace Wyndham Goldie thought that if the programme was finally decided upon the right person as producer should be Stephen Hearst who had just done a very successful programme in the East. I came away from Television Centre that afternoon feeling rather hopeful that the Greek programme would materialise.

I needed all the optimism I could muster to deal with the Income Tax situation. The trouble I had with the Inspector of Taxes when I moved from the Channel Islands to Scotland was being repeated in Edinburgh after I moved there from Berkshire. Income Tax Inspectors always believe that authors are making much more money than they admit. I do not blame Inspectors so much for this as authors. It has to be realised that very few authors tell the truth about their circulation. They cannot help exaggerating. I am grateful to the one-eighth puritan in my composition; I believe it is that which prevents my own exaggerating.

My state of mind is revealed in these extracts from letters.

On April 5 Chrissie wrote to Faith:

"We are having a worrying time here trying to get Income Tax returns in shape. The Inspector is being alarming with suggestions that there is money hidden away somewhere, perhaps in Italy or Greece! Then he suggests that all the money from broadcasting and journalism has not been returned etc., etc. All this when he is trying to get *Rockets Galore* finished. He badly needs a rest and if he can finish his book he will enjoy his short visit to Lady Eldon and it will do him good. On the whole he's keeping fairly free from pain apart from pain in his left palm through holding down the page proofs of 'Sublime Tobacco' which have just been finished and sent off. It is staggering and how he does it all is a miracle. I don't believe any other writer of his age does it. But this taxation is crippling. At times of greater exasperation with it all he says 'I really must leave this so and so country and live abroad'. Of course it soon passes—but I have heard it said more than once."

To Faith I was writing two days later:

I'm having a hell of a difficult time with the Income Tax people. . . .

I'm driving myself hard to finish 'Rockets Galore' but I don't think I will have it finished for press before my Easter Vac of a week with Jack and Magdalen Eldon. I have to be back here to reply for 'Education' at the Conference dinner of the National Association of Schoolmasters. Then finish off Rockets and get back at once to 'Mezzotint'.

I do hope you'll have a successful villegiatura in Italy. . . . And don't worry about my I.T. problems. I shall survive somehow.

One of the novels I may manage to write is waiting its turn. It will be the story of a Treasury spy called *Tell Tale Tit*.

Somebody had written to tell me that I must be less casual over business matters and I wrote back:

"When one is working a 12 hour day with a single eye, and that obscured by cataract, in one's 75th year one becomes pretty casual about everything but one's work. I am coming to the conclusion that it will be impossible for me to go on living in Edinburgh because my position here as the doyen of Scottish writers involves me in social demands and consequently heavy expenses that a few months' illness could make it impossible for me to meet.

"I shall not be able to afford as expensive a move as it was coming here, and I shall have to sell the greater part of my library. I don't suppose the I.T. people will give way over my expenses claim for that move, but I just refused again to accept their offer of half. All or nothing!"

By now the reader is possibly as anxious to get away from Income Tax problems as I was. By the time I had reached Taunton on that Wednesday of Holy Week I had forgotten that such a thing as Income Tax existed.

One of the pleasures of that delightful week was meeting Hugh Fraser's beautiful young wife Antonia. She was on the way to producing her eldest daughter Rebecca. I recall travelling back with them in the train to London.

Back in Edinburgh after that tonic week I was glad to get a letter from Grace Wyndham Goldie which made me feel fairly confident that the Greek programme was a genuine likelihood. Stephen Hearst, the young producer, was to come and discuss the programme with me in June when he returned from a documentary he was making abroad.

Meanwhile, another very attractive possibility appeared on the scene. Stanley Jackson had asked me on my way through London if I would be interested in writing the script for a screen play which Herbert Wilcox hoped to make. Leslie Howard was to be the principal figure and it was to be called *Flight 777*.

On May 18th Herbert Wilcox wrote from 12 Aldford House, Park Lane:

"Stanley Jackson has advised me of his discussion with you and I hasten to assure you I have no intention of introducing any alien element in the screen play of FLIGHT 777.

"I am sure that with your appreciation of entertainment value, you realise suspense and an element of surprise must be brought into the screen play to hold the interest of audiences who are in advance aware of the climax.

"In producing NURSE EDITH CAVELL, ODETTE and THE

STORY OF H.M.S. AMETHYST I was faced with the same problem of inevitability and the critical acclaim and success of the pictures demonstrated that the licence taken was acceptable.

"In the case of LESLIE HOWARD, we have the susceptibilities of his family—apart from relatives of other participants to consider.

"Of course we had to face this problem in the AMETHYST story and with the immediate relatives of ODETTE CHURCHILL and NURSE CAVELL. I have omitted mentioning QUEEN VICTORIA since the widespread problems in that case must be obvious.

"I assure you my honest approach to the subject matches your own but I share your fears that a straight narration of the events would not carry the necessary excitement or entertainment value.

"My thought when first approaching you to write the screen play arose from a profound regard for your work (dating back to SIN-ISTER STREET) and the fact that you would introduce some of your inside knowledge of the Secret Service and its workings which obviously was an important element in the tragedy.

"Whilst fixing attention primarily on Leslie Howard, I feel certain other characters can be linked with the flight; also the chance postponement to show 'The first of the few' can be dramatised on a fatalistic note.

"I understand from Stanley Jackson I am fortunate in finding you immediately available to undertake the writing of the screen play but would like a meeting with me before finally agreeing to do so.

"I cannot leave London until Thursday next as I am involved in the finishing processes of a new picture but if agreeable to you I can come up on Thursday night and meet you Friday morning in Edinburgh.

With warmest regards.

Yours sincerely,
Herbert Wilcox."

Herbert Wilcox came up to discuss the project in Edinburgh, and we found ourselves in complete agreement about the way to treat the screen play. I got down to work on it as soon as possible and at the beginning of July Wilcox came up again to hear me read it to him.

"I could put this on the floor tomorrow," he exclaimed and I can still see his look of surprise. "The only pity is that you won't be able to play every part."

Herbert Wilcox was never able to produce *Flight 777* because the widow and son of Leslie Howard were unwilling to co-operate and without that co-operation it would have been impossible to proceed.

Herbert Wilcox and I also discussed a film of *Water on the Brain*. That came to nothing as indeed every other proposal to make a film of *Water on the Brain* has come to nothing. Whitehall dislikes being laughed at. Proposals to film *The Red Tapeworm* have been equally discouraged.

Stephen Hearst came up to see me about the Greek programme which it was proposed to call *The Glory that was Greece*.

"And we might follow that up," I suggested, "with *The Grandeur that was Rome*."

As I remember Stephen Hearst was booked up for this year, and I told him I should take advantage of an invitation I had received from Swan's Hellenic Cruises to accompany a cruise toward the end of August as a guest lecturer. At the same time a Greek sent me an Olympic Airways ticket to Athens and back. I decided that if I accepted the latter I should be suspected of some desperate mission connected with the state of affairs in Cyprus and decided that a less conspicuous return to Greece on an Aegean cruise would be a wiser course. I expected to hear from the B.B.C. when Stephen Hearst went back, but I heard nothing, and made up my mind that *The Glory that was Greece* was just another iridescent bubble that would presently burst.

A bubble that did not burst was a film of *Rockets Galore* by Pinewood Films. News of this just when Anthony Bradshaw and I were in the throes of what in a letter to Faith on July 27 I called *A hectic 3 days with I.T. and our accountant, but I think things will smooth themselves out. The problem now is to spread the money from 'Rockets Galore' in order to avoid more than half of it being collared for supertax.*

Those battles with the Inland Revenue are now battles of long ago and old far-off unhappy things and since 1957, thanks to my accountant, there has not been even a mild skirmish.

In that letter to Faith I was writing *Lily is getting on well at the hairdressers. She was determined to justify Strachan's perception when he engaged her. Already she is as quick as younger girls who have been two years at the job. She will remain there for at least a year.*

I was glad to see Donald Wolfit's name in the Birthday Honours this summer and I wrote my congratulations. I had met him for the first time in the previous year and in his company I had been back

in the theatre of once upon a time. Here is his reply from the Garrick
Club that July:

*How WONDERFULLY kind of you to write—your letter has made me
very happy.*

Do you remember Phil May's Cartoon in 1895 of the old pro landlady.

*'Yuss, I'm glad they've gone and knighted Enery Irving. You see, it's a
compliment to the perfession which reflecks h'equal 'onner on us hall.'*

*Let us hope that in the next few years I can do something to earn it. If
only I could persuade 'Winnie' to help with the bricklaying we might get a
National Theatre up in a year.*

*Alas, I missed your visit to the Garrick but you left an aura of good taste
that hung around for days.*

*Long life and happiness to you. I shall always remember our evening last
year.*

Yours
Donald Wolfit

There was still no news of that proposed TV programme *The
Glory that was Greece* when I set out toward the end of August to
join the *Adriatiki* at Venice for that Aegean cruise.

I have written at some length in *Greece in my Life* of my emotion
at revisiting Hellas after forty years and I shall not dwell upon them
again. When I found that my cabin was Z I hoped it was a good
omen for my return to Greece next year for that TV project, and
I took it also as a sign that I should keep quiet about my revisiting
Hellas because I knew I should have reporters wherever the ship
stopped asking me about the state of affairs in Cyprus. I had
received the thanks of the City of Athens for my poor efforts to
obtain as much as a fair hearing for the Cyprus case. The Athens
Press had given me the epithet once given to Aristides—the just—
and I did not want to be ostracised because some readers were tired
of hearing my name prefaced by that epithet.

I could not resist the opportunity of visiting Delphi for the first
time and I must indulge myself in one brief quotation from *Greece
in my Life* because it was for me one of the thrills of a lifetime:

"A faint irritation of climbing the Sacred Way for the first time
in a crowd was abruptly dispelled by the music of the two nightingales singing to each other in a thicket of Parnassus. I played with
the fancy that those two birds which at April's end or in the front
of May had been bewitching the night in Hampshire or in Hert-
fordshire, had arrived home from their stay in England and were so

glad to be safely back that they could not keep from song although it was the season of the year when birdsong is mute. I never heard nightingales pour out such a cascade of liquid music under the moon as they were pouring out now with the sun blazing overhead. Enelpides in The Birds of Aristophanes might have cried:

> O sovereign Zeus, the voice of that little bird!
> It has made honey-sweet the whole thicket."

I was back in Edinburgh early in September and greatly relieved to hear from Tony Bradshaw that H.M.'s Inspector of Taxes had suggested that the Inland Revenue would allow me five-sixths of the move from Berkshire as expenses if I accepted the other sixth as a personal expense.

Since Thin Ice was published I had been receiving letters from homosexuals who felt that I had presented their handicap fairly to those who were not suffering from such a handicap. The publication of the Wolfenden Report naturally produced a volume of uncomprehending comment. One letter I received is worth preserving to show what the reception of the Wolfenden Report was in some quarters:

"I expect you saw the farrago of old wives' tales which the Daily Mail served up this morning as an Editorial on the Wolfenden Report. Its main contentions (that freedom would cause an immediate increase in homosexuality and that homosexuality 'caused the decline and fall of ancient civilisations') are refuted in the Report itself. Furthermore the Mail quotes the 'scare' figure of 6000 convictions a year, whereas the Report makes it plain that for the private actions of consenting adults the average is 160 annual convictions."

The writer went on to ask if a few people like Lord Brabazon and myself would protest against the Daily Mail's distortion of the Wolfenden Report. I felt I had enough on my hands with the Cyprus state of affairs and the misguided missiles of South Uist to enter into the controversy about the Wolfenden Report. I had tried in Thin Ice to give a fair picture of the effect of homosexuality on the career of a public man, and I had at the back of my mind one more novel about it. That novel has not yet been written but when this last Octave of My Life and Times is finished I may turn to it as my next job.

There was a Rectorial Election in Edinburgh that October for which Malcolm Muggeridge was one of the candidates. He had recently written a rather foolish article in which he had said that the U people were inclined to criticise the Queen's style of dressing but that the typists and shopgirls thought she was beautifully dressed. The *Sunday Express* came out with a front-page article with banner headlines proclaiming that Malcolm Muggeridge had said the Queen was dowdy.

The immediate effect of that front page in the *Sunday Express* was that the *Sunday Dispatch* broke their contract with Muggeridge to write for them a weekly article and the B.B.C. banned him from appearing in television or broadcasting.

When Malcolm Muggeridge came along to see me I told him I thought it was a mistake to offer oneself as a future Rector unless one had a chance of polling more than a hundred votes. Malcolm told me that he had quite an enthusiastic lot of supporters.

"If you poll a hundred you'll be lucky," I told him. "James Robertson Justice is almost sure to be elected."

In fact Malcolm Muggeridge received exactly one hundred votes and James Justice was elected by a substantial majority.

Then I went on:

"Are you suing the *Sunday Express* for libel, Malcolm?"

Malcolm looked surprised by my question.

"No, I hadn't thought of doing so. I think it's best to ignore that kind of thing."

"But damn it, Malcolm, you can show actual financial damage for that article. In most libel actions damages are awarded without the plaintiff's being able to show any actual financial loss. You can show heavy losses. The *Dispatch* sacked you from what must have been at least a fifteen hundred a year job, and the B.B.C. have banned you. For heaven's sake throw in a writ for libel. Subpoena various people to testify for you. Subpoena me for one. I will go into the witness-box and your counsel will ask me what was my impression after reading that article in the *Sunday Express*. I shall reply: 'My impression was that my friend Malcolm Muggeridge had gone off his rocker.'

"Your counsel will then ask: 'But when you read in *The Times*, *The Scotsman* and *The Manchester Guardian* exactly what my client actually wrote what was your impression then?'

"And I shall reply: 'It went to confirm what I have for some time suspected, that it was the policy of Lord Beaverbrook to cheapen the effect of royalty in the interest of popular journalism.'"

When Malcolm Muggeridge returned to the South he wrote a

letter to say that he was going to take my advice and sue for libel. Perhaps other people dissuaded him. At any rate, instead of suing for libel he complained to the Press Council. I do not recall whether the Press Council censured the *Express*. If they did it was probably as tepid a reproof as usual.

Some years later Malcolm Muggeridge was elected Rector of Edinburgh University and stood up to the hairy fairies of a small student minority. He was asked to preach in St Giles and delivered a remarkable sermon in which he denounced the various pep drugs with the eloquence and fervour of a Savonarola. Then, inexplicably to me, he resigned his Rectorship, and the University lost a Rector who was not prepared to surrender to the absurdities of youth in order to seem younger than he was.

Charles Eade retired that autumn from the editorial chair of the *Sunday Dispatch* in which he had sat for nineteen years. I told in Octave 5 the story of the serialisation of *The Windsor Tapestry* after Hugh Cudlipp's attempt to present himself as a synthetic Puritan in the *Sunday Pictorial*. In the formal letter from Carmelite House announcing his retirement Charles Eade had added a postscript in his own hand:

Let us never forget my first big winner with 'The Windsor Tapestry'. What a triumph that was!

Neither Charles Eade nor the *Sunday Dispatch* is still with us in 1970.

In 1956 the City Fathers of Edinburgh had committed a savage act of vandalism without a word of warning to the residents of Drummond Place. Gangs of workmen had arrived to knock down the lamp-posts with their beautiful copper gas-lamps and erected in their place ghastly concrete electrical gibbets, the light of which take all the colour out of the painting of the doors and windows. We had protested with sufficient noise to consider ourselves responsible for saving the lamp-posts of Heriot Row and Moray Place from destruction.

I find a letter presumably written to *The Scotsman* in December 1957 on the subject of Edinburgh traffic:

"When Mr Morris from his little bicycle shop in High Street, Oxford bought a piece of the old covered market and hoisted the sign (still there) Morris's Oxford Garage it was for me the writing on the wall and vainly I urged the construction of what is now called a by-pass round Oxford. My apprehensions were derided in 1903 as a piece of undergraduate extravagance, but Oxford has been

destroyed by Lord Nuffield and his like. They have made pande-
monium; they call it progress. Now the alarm bell that Mr Moray
McLaren's letter has sounded in my head persuades me to expose
myself once again to the taunt of extravagance.

"I should have realised last year when a few civic vandals erected
those disgusting lamp-posts in Drummond Place and Great King
Street that there was more behind the business than mere lack of
taste. Let one of the City Fathers come forward at once and give us
a solemn assurance that he and his colleagues are not conspiring to
destroy the New Town to save five minutes inconvenience for
motorists.

"If the problem of Edinburgh traffic is as serious as the City
Fathers believe it to be let them tackle the antiquated transport of
British Railways and demand the destruction of the Waverley and
Princes Street stations and the conversion of the railway-line between
them into a road wide enough to park cars along both sides of it.
Haymarket and Abbeyhill will serve railway users equally well
during the comparatively few years that railways will be in exist-
ence."

Since then Princes Street station has become extinct but instead
of taking advantage of that to build an opera house and a new
Caledonian Hotel those infernal ant-heaps of reinforced concrete
are going up, and in a few years the Modern Athens will be as foul
an architectural horror as modern London is rapidly becoming.

At the end of this year my association with Grant's Standfast
whisky was renewed and has continued ever since. For me it has
been invaluable and for the generosity with which I have been
treated I find it difficult to express my gratitude. However, I can
say with absolute sincerity that the task of writing these ten Octaves
of *My Life and Times* has been continuously lightened by the good-
will of Grants.

By the end of the year I had long decided that the project of
The Glory that was Greece for television was yet another bubble. I
fancied that the Swan cruise this summer would be my last farewell to Greece. Then suddenly in that December I received a letter
from the B.B.C. which set me off blowing bubbles again, all richly
iridescent. It was suggested that Stephen Hearst should come up
to Edinburgh in the New Year and that in association with him
I should write the details of a programme for three television
hours.

By now Faith's lease of the flat in Sheffield Terrace was coming to an end, and the rent for another lease was to be trebled. I suggested that we should make the sub-basement into a comfortable flat for her. She would be eighty next February. If she went out to Italy until April she would be able to finish her book about Bagni di Lucca and the British colony there.

F AITH had gone to Capri early in January with my niece Jean Howard on some business the reason for which I cannot remember. I was writing to her on the day before my seventy-fifth birthday to thank her for a birthday telegram:

I have been having a hectic week between trying to get on with 'The Lunatic Republic', grapple with the film-script of 'Rockets Galore' and dealing with a mass of urgent correspondence.

I am relieved to hear that you think Capri is doing you good. I was worried by your last letter. I know the thought is a gloomy one for you, but you will be eighty next month and we shall have to decide soon whether you are going on living alone in Sheffield Terrace or whether you will have your own flat in Drummond Place. Any kind of building alterations takes ages nowadays. Chrissie will be writing to you the details of the proposed garden flat in our sub-basement. At the moment she and Lily are submerged in preparations for the birthday party tomorrow.

I received rather a nice birthday present today from the Irvine Burns Club to say I had been unanimously elected an honorary member at their annual general meeting, the qualification for which is to be "a distinguished poet, a man of national eminence or a special benefactor of the Club". I was asked to reply in my own handwriting so that my letter could be added to the holograph collection begun when the Club was founded in 1826. These include Sir Walter Scott, Wordsworth, Dickens, Tennyson, Garibaldi, Gladstone, Winston Churchill, Eisenhower, the Duke of Edinburgh and Mountbatten.

By the same post I heard that the Authors' Club has made me President in succession to Dunsany.

James Justice's mother stayed with us for her son's installation as Rector of the University. Of that remarkable woman Chrissie wrote to Faith:

"She is a pet and a terrific gardener. She moved 40 tons of flint last year from her garden in Hampshire (Nether Wallop) in a wheelbarrow. She says that apart from a bad knee it doesn't seem to have done her any harm. She played your piano and says it badly needs playing on. But this you know and we are all looking forward to your playing on it yourself."

The Duke of Edinburgh was a friend of James Justice and had been much interested in his falconry. As Chancellor of the University

C.M. and Lily at the time of their marriage

31 Drummond Place

The entrance hall of 31 Drummond Place

he had come up to Edinburgh to preside at the Installation. James was in good form and handled the occasional good humoured interrupters during his address always with effect. Two or three rolls of toilet-paper came floating down from the gallery to the platform one of which twisted itself round Prince Philip without his appearing to notice it.

There is no doubt that familiarity with acting either on the stage or in films or television is of great service to a Rector facing the students at his installation. My Rectorial at Glasgow with Alastair Sim's and James Justice's at Edinburgh were lullabies compared with what various political Rectors have had to endure, the most outrageous example of which was to happen in Glasgow the day after James Justice's Rectorial when R. A. Butler[1] was installed as Rector of that University.

I forget if James was chaired by his supporters after the ceremony; if he was it must have been something of a test for youthful muscles.

It had been decided that after his visit to the Women's Union the Royal Chancellor would have a quiet hour at 31 Drummond Place before attending the big dinner with its speeches and going on afterwards to the Union before taking the night train back to London. It was imperative to conceal the Duke's visit from reporters and camera-men, partly for his own relaxation and partly because I did not want to advertise the favour to 31 Drummond Place. We were successful in keeping the secret and while the press and camera-men were chasing one clue after another all over Edinburgh, the Duke himself, his equerry and the new Rector of the University were enjoying an old malt whisky given to me by Grants and uncorked for the occasion.

Nadina, the five-year-old daughter of Jack and Delia Lennie, was very anxious to see what a Prince looked like outside a fairy story. Prince Philip was gracious enough to receive the curtsey of that half-Scottish, half-Italian wee lass, and Nadina was far more at ease than most debutantes at their first Court. Nadina wrote to her aunt in Rome about the event and wound up by recording that the Prince's hair was very tidy.

It does not surprise me that Prince Philip enjoyed hawking with James Justice: he himself can strike like a hawk from time to time at British slowness of motion.

I had written to Rab Butler to apologise for not being able to

[1] Rt. Hon. Lord Butler of Saffron Walden.

attend his Rectorial at Glasgow owing to my having to attend the Rectorial Installation at Edinburgh the preceding day.

I now wrote to express my disgust at the way he had been treated by the Glasgow students who, apart from howling like a pack of dogs, had poured bucket after bucket of flour over him. In his letter to me the Rector of Glasgow University described his abominable experience with typical moderation as an "unfortunate half-hour".

What in my opinion the country lost when the premiership was not offered to Lord Butler, Trinity College has gained. He was almost the only Chancellor of the Exchequer who seemed ever to have read a book, looked at a picture or listened to a note of music. He was almost the only Chancellor of the Exchequer who did as much as he could to change the irresponsible way in which authors were being taxed. His election as President of the Royal Society of Literature was an invigoration.

To my great relief Faith decided that she would give up Sheffield Terrace in June and live in the flat I proposed to put in order for her at 31 Drummond Place. I felt that even the exasperatingly slow builders of the time might manage to transform the sub-basement within four months.

That February certainly was a bright month in my life in spite of a good deal of pain. Two days after James Justice's successful Rectorial I received a letter from the B.B.C. that was indeed a welcome surprise.

"I am sorry that it should have taken us so long to reach a decision on 'The Glory that was Greece' but we are delighted to be able to write to you and say that the whole project has now been approved.

"We are most grateful for your draft treatment, which gave a very good idea of your approach to this project, and we have very high hopes that these three films, although undoubtedly expensive, will have the success we expect.

"If you agree, the three films will be shot in October and November of this year, the producer Stephen Hearst, having consulted you in spring and summer and having gone ahead to Greece in September to prepare shooting scripts. I would be very grateful if you could let us know whether the months of October and November would be convenient to you and will then ask for a contract to be drawn up in respect of the series."

I managed to finish *The Lunatic Republic* before going down to

London at the beginning of April to do some television and broadcasting for which I had been booked.

One of these was to appear in a series called *Speaking Personally*. This was a severe test of the speaker's ability to sound as if he was in the room and not in a television studio. There one was alone without any introduction by sight or sound. My predecessors on this programme had tried hard to appear spontaneous without succeeding. That *Speaking Personally* was the only time I have felt a hint of stage fright on television. I felt I had failed to carry off *Speaking Personally*.

Few letters have given me so much pleasure as one I had from Lord Mountbatten:

"*My dear Mackenzie*,

I am very sorry that we missed your broadcast on television last night which I am told was outstanding. I gather you made some very kind and flattering remarks about us which I am sure were not fully justified but for which we are nevertheless very grateful; but what interests me most is that I hear you made some very fine remarks on the transfer of power in August, 1947, with particular reference to Lord Attlee and Gandhiji—finally following up with a tribute to the Indian Army.

"Of course we know full well that you who were on the spot at the time appreciate only too well all that we were trying to do for the good of this country and India over ten years ago—all with the full support and backing of Lord Attlee. But there are all too many people in this country who still cannot see the wisdom of that imaginative act of 15th August, 1947, and we could not let your broadcast pass without expressing our gratitude for all that you said so broadly and clearly about the transfer of power and which cannot fail to have made a great impact on the millions who will have seen and heard you.

"With all good wishes from us both.

> *Yours very sincerely,*
> *Mountbatten of Burma*"

There was another which would give equal pleasure ten years afterwards. Before going to France in 1968 I had recorded a long talk for radio with Patrick Harvey. This was put out by the B.B.C. in a programme called something like *A Year I Remember* and lasted for nearly an hour. I never heard it myself but the year being recalled was 1947. I was much moved by a letter most kindly sent to me just after Lord Attlee died. In it I was told that it was the last broadcast to which Attlee had listened just before he went into hospital and that my tribute to him had given much pleasure. I was grateful for that letter, humbly I hope.

Back to 1958. It was in this summer that Rosamond Lehmann received a telegram from Bali to say that her beloved only daughter Sally Kavanagh had died from polio. A day or two later came a letter from Sally telling about the wonderful time she was having in Bali and how she was enjoying every moment of it. I am left without words. Those who have read about that enchanting god-daughter of mine in earlier Octaves will know what a shock that tragedy was. The courage with which Rosamond bore herself in her desolation was truly heroic. Sally's husband, P. J. Kavanagh wrote *The Perfect Stranger*, a profoundly moving book about that happy marriage so cruelly broken.

Two letters from James Thurber bring back a wonderful night at the Stafford Hotel in St James's Place:

"Dear Monty,
Helen and I were delighted to get your note and to know that you are coming South in July. We shall be here between the 15th and 23rd, waiting for you.

"We want to bring you to the Stafford for dinner and whisky and the evening, either keeping you to ourselves or sharing you with whomever you would like to see that we could get hold of.

"I am especially interested in having Joe Sayre, a fine and lusty American writer, meet you. Like all of us Americans worthy of the name, he knows and loves your work. He was at Oxford in the early '20's and recently wrote a fascinating piece about revisiting it for the New Yorker.

"I am finishing my book on Harold Ross, which will take all of July, and we won't be able to come to Edinburgh this year.

"We do count on seeing you, and please assure us in a brief sentence that you will come to see us.
Love from us both.
As always,
James"

I suggested Friday 18th as a possible date to meet to which he replied:

"Friday the 18th will be perfect for Helen and me, and we shall look forward to seeing you here at the Stafford Hotel around 8 o'clock that evening.

"Joe Sayre is most anxious to be here to meet you, but he has been to Oxford for the Gawdy and is going back there again the day after tomorrow. He does hope to be here on Friday the 18th.

"If you should like to see Jamie Hamilton too, I think he will be here at the time, but I shall await your word about that. Yvonne will be in Italy, so he will be on his own in London.

"I have only written a fourth as many books as you have, but complain four times as much about the burden of finishing a book. It has taken me exactly a year to near the end of my brief history of the crazy New Yorker and its lunatic editor. Or maybe they are sane and I have gone out of my mind.

"Anyway, I know that you will restore me to sanity.

Affectionately,

James"

In that August Elsie Maxwell[1] left us. Readers of Octave 8 will know how much I admired her wisdom and dauntless vitality. As I write these words I am sitting beside her on the big sofa in Moray Place talking about the lilies she loved and about which she wrote a splendid book when she was in her eighties. In *The Times* I wrote:

"The death of the Hon. Mrs Constable-Maxwell on Thursday has taken from this world one of the most remarkable women of our time. Those who had been privileged to enjoy her friendship have the feeling of dismay when somebody young, loved by the gods, is taken from us. She was in her eighty-ninth year, but so alert was her vitality, so quick was her comprehension, and so bright was her glance that the only mark she showed of age was her wisdom.

"Only three or four years ago she wrote a book about lilies which is a *sine qua non* for anybody who wants to cultivate those lovely flowers. Such a feat of concentration was nothing less than astounding, for it involved infinite care and continuous exactitude. Every reference was verified; there was not a single slip throughout a book of practical information, the compiling of which would have taxed the industry of an enthusiastic gardener in his prime.

"For the last three years she had been at work on memoirs of her long past and recording some of the history of the families, so rich

[1] The Hon. Mrs Bernard Constable-Maxwell.

in romance, from which she sprang. Almost to the very end she was absorbed in correcting that labour of love.

"Mrs Constable-Maxwell was a sister of the late Lord Lovat, the widow of the Hon. Bernard Constable-Maxwell, and the mother of six sons and six daughters. She could have been a matriarch in the grand style, but in fact she was much more like the eldest sister of a large family.

"I, who enjoyed her friendship for nearly thirty years, have never known any woman more interested in other people and less interested in herself; conversation with her was always an enchanting lesson in objectivity. Her sympathy with youth was boundless; she made none of those demands on others which old age too often makes when self-indulgence becomes less easy to achieve.

"She was the fine flower of aristocracy, but it is significant that, of those resplendent lilies about which she wrote so well, the one she loved best was the white martagon, the simplest of them all."

Stephen Hearst went off to Greece at the end of that August to prepare the way for the three 40-minute films he was to produce and in which I was to take part. He wrote from Athens at the beginning of September:

"The magic of your philhellenism has created a climate of opinion so favourable' that all the planning and preparation in the world would avail nothing without it if we are to finish three films in the time allotted. We have had generous help with motor transport. George Kavounides, the Director of the Foreign Press Division of the Greek Government, has engineered marvellous short cuts through administrative mazes. We are getting the loan of a military aircraft to film Mount Olympus from the air with the outstanding Greek cameraman Basil Maros to do it. The Press have given us a lot of coverage, and of course when you arrive you'll get interviews galore. I confess I was a little apprehensive about our reception at this time of tension when the papers are full of blood-curdling descriptions of British wickedness but all the people here have been marvellously kind and helpful. If only the weather is kind when we start filming."

Chrissie and I reached Athens from Heathrow about three weeks later. Stephen announced that he had arranged for us to join a small party going to the wine festival at Daphne that night. I wondered if the wine festival was a plan to test my stamina and reassure himself about my ability to ride up a mountainside on a mule. If after a flight from Heathrow to Athens I could sit on an uncomfortable chair in a crowded babel until two in the morning without showing signs of undue fatigue, he could hope that I should be able to reach the birthplace of Zeus on Mount Dictys and face the camera at the entrance of the cave. I survived the test; in fact it was Stephen's inside that was upset by the wine festival. I may add that later on in Crete I was successful in riding a mule up to the cave on Mount Dictys in which Zeus was born. This was about 4000 feet. What is more I rode down again without falling off.

Next day I tried to revisit the scenes of those exciting fifteen months I had spent in Athens so long ago. The landmarks had vanished. The old British Legation had gone. The Annexe had gone. The Ministry of Finance opposite had gone. My house in Ghizi Street of which the Constantinists had made a pepper-pot with bullets was not even a pinch of pepper today. The old house in Visarionos Street was gone, buried beneath a towering office building.

Charles de Jaeger and Johnny Ray arrived with the camera equipment and we set off for Crete. With us went Milto Spyromilios who had been a friend of Stephen Hearst's father. He acted as a kind of dragoman to Stephen when he was dashing about all over Greece before Chrissie and I arrived. He stayed with us throughout all three films and was invaluable as guide, philosopher and friend. He was an Epirote of ancient lineage whose great-grandfather was killed at Missolonghi.

One of the pleasures of those crowded seven weeks in Crete and the mainland of Greece was to meet for the first time Patrick Leigh Fermor after having driven along the road in Crete where he took a leading part in capturing the German General. I found him as much a man after my own heart as from his books I had expected to find him. He did not resemble Norman Douglas either in looks or conversation but his company brought back the mood of days spent with Norman Douglas more nearly than anybody has done. Chrissie and I dined with him in his favourite *taverna* where I was surrounded by cats whose optimism about tit-bits I did not disappoint.

Patrick Leigh Fermor was with us on the day we reached Thermopylae.

"The last time I saw Thermopylae," he said, "was with a British army in hurried retreat. Not a pretty sight."

It caught my heart to stand upon that mound where the Three Hundred gave their lives to delay the Persian advance and read with emotion the immortal epitaph upon that slab:

Take a message, stranger, to the Lacedemonians, that obedient to their word we lie here.

At the base of the mound many cyclamens were in flower.

Back in Athens I went to see Archbishop Makarios and was greatly impressed by him. That murder of a British sergeant's wife had occurred about ten days before and the Archbishop had been much upset by it. It had nothing whatever to do with EOKA but of course some British newspapers liked to suggest that it had in order to work up the emotions of their readers. I told the Archbishop that I thought it would be wise to relinquish the demand for *enosis*, and now. I also said how much Cypriot well-wishers hoped that terrorist murder would not begin again.

I saw the Archbishop again three weeks later and said I hoped he was not counting too much on action by the United Nations. My own belief was that the Americans would exercise their influence behind the scenes in New York to prevent the question of Cyprus being raised.

"Like ourselves", I went on, "they have a pathetic belief in the power and influence of Turkey in the Near and Middle East. The Turks took advantage of the Cyprus dispute to obtain more money, more material and more arms. I can't help feeling that if Greece and Turkey get together without interruptions from Great Britain and the United States they could come to terms. Anyway if UNO does let you down I wish you would ponder the possibility of coming to an arrangement with the Turks. The Sandjak of Alexandretta may offer them a nasty problem if they press too hard for partition in Cyprus. Only a six to four majority for Turks over Syrians."

The Archbishop's secretary came in to ask if the cameramen could take a photograph, and the Archbishop, who was in archepiscopal negligé, was arrayed in hat and staff and proper vestments to be photographed with me. I still see the Archbishop in episcopal negligé and hear the tone of his voice as he murmurs almost wistfully:

"I think that Lord Harding was beginning to understand the state of affairs in Cyprus. Like myself he came from simple people."

And then the Archbishop said with what was nearer to a grin than a smile:

"Mr Lennox Boyd sent me to the Seychelles with another bishop and two priests."

He did not seem to hold the slightest resentment against the

Colonial Secretary. It was obvious that he regarded his handling of the situation in Cyprus foolish enough to be comic.

I think it was at the end of September before the murder of the soldier's wife in Nicosia that I met Barbara Castle at the Grande-Bretagne Hotel with Mrs Jeger and other Labour M.P.s. She showed moral courage, and indeed physical courage of the highest order by going to Cyprus and defending EOKA against the accusation of the murder. For this she was almost reviled by the popular Press, which at this date was feeding the ignorance of the British public with bloodthirsty trash.

I told the Archbishop that every fresh murder now would hand votes to the Conservatives at another General Election. Nobody was more anxious than the Archbishop to call a halt to violence, but the clumsy way in which he had been exploited as the chief villain had made it impossible for him to give a public statement about violence without being accused of surrender. The most he could do to bring the intolerable situation to an end was to surrender the demand for *enosis*, and this at whatever cost to his own hopes he did. Pandit Nehru made a similar surrender when he accepted the partition of India in 1947 and at least he had the satisfaction of knowing that Lord Attlee and Lord Mountbatten appreciated that such a surrender was an act of self-abnegation.

I reminded the Archbishop that Crete had had to wait fourteen years for *enosis* after the island was liberated from Turkish rule in 1898, and that even if he had to wait twice as long he would still be two years younger than I who was talking to him.

Before leaving Athens on November 15th, I gave a broadcast in which I naturally avoided saying anything about the handling of Cyprus by the Conservative Government. I did feel justified, however, in asking the Turks if they had sufficiently considered what might be the effect on President Nasser of partition in Cyprus. I reminded them that the proportion of Turks over Syrians in the Sandjak of Alexandretta was only six to four compared with four to one of Greeks over Turks in Cyprus. "And if", I said, "the United Arab Republic decided to press for partition in Alexandretta that could all too easily lead to a third world war."

On the same day as I left Athens for London Archbishop Makarios left Athens for New York for the fifth appeal to the United Nations to intervene over Cyprus. The appeal was rejected largely by American influence; the United States did not want all its aid to Turkey to be money thrown away. And then soon after the New Year representatives of the Greek and Turkish Governments got together at Zürich and produced a *modus vivendi*, in the course of arriving at which the Greeks seemed to have sacrificed a good deal more than the Turks. The impossibility of co-existence in Cyprus between the two was shown to be a convenient pretence. Communal strife never existed until the Conservative Government invented it as an excuse for opposing independence. Those who know anything about the Near East during this century, and their number does not include a high proportion of politicians called upon to provide for its future, know that the danger to the Republic of Cyprus lies in the struggle for power between Left and Right. It is fortunate that the Cypriots have a man in the prime of life as Ethnarch. *Orandum est ut sit mens sana in corpore sano.* Let us pray for a healthy mind in a healthy body. Doctors are powerful enough today without making men of state dependent on them.

Before the departure of the plane in which Chrissie and I were flying to Heathrow many Greek friends came to wish us goodbye and I was presented with eight bottles of various Greek wines and spirits. I explained to the Customs officer at Heathrow why I had all these bottles.

"Whisky Galore," he replied with a benign grin and they were waved on duty free.

I told in Octave Two of the customs officer at Southampton who spoilt my butterflies by forcing open in the rain the cigar-boxes in which they were pinned. That benign grin from a customs officer sixty-four years later was full compensation.

The day after I returned from Greece there was a photograph of me shaking hands with Archbishop Makarios at the Athens airport and presently I was interviewed by the *Daily Mail* and said that I believed from the evidence I had heard in Greece that the murder of the British sergeant's wife in Nicosia had been committed by a Turk.

The Turkish Press Attaché protested to the *Daily Mail* and I received a letter from the Chairman of the Cyprus-is-Turkish Association in London:

"19th November, 1958.
"Sir,

You should be ashamed of yourself in making such an irresponsible statement as the one we read in the Daily Mail on 17th November.

"How dare you blame the Turkish Cypriots for the murder of

Mrs ——? What evidence have you got to prove that? You may well be bought by the Greeks, but you have no right to sell the Turks to them as well.

"Not even a single British soul was shot by the Turks in Cyprus. On the contrary, since the beginning of terrorism, nearly 200 Turkish people have been killed by EOKA. Most of the victims were policemen helping the British in their fight against terrorism.

"Surely that is not the kind of praise we expect from people like you in return. Your statement can serve no purpose other than agitating the Turkish Cypriots to start killing the British. That, of course, would be very dangerous and grave.

"May I advise you, therefore, that in future if you cannot make any utterance to serve a useful purpose, it would be best for you to shut up."

I sent the following reply to the *Daily Mail*:

"23rd November, 1958.

"Sir,

What I said and what the *Daily Mail* accurately reported was that I believed a Turk was responsible for the murder of a British woman in Cyprus. I now reaffirm that belief for these reasons:

"1. There was no possible advantage to the Greek cause in Cyprus for such a beastly action.

"2. Eoka immediately disavowed any responsibility for it.

"3. If, as they claim, the British Security forces now know all the members of Eoka why has no evidence been offered that the murder was perpetrated by a member of Eoka?

"4. The bootlicking of Turkey in which the present British and United States Governments are indulging demands, if it were known that such a detestable murder had been committed by a Turk that neither the British nor the American people should be told.

"5. If Eoka's denial of guilt is not believed, why is not Eoka challenged to denounce the murderer who committed this crime against orders?

"6. It is the Turkish policy to feed bitterness in Cyprus in order to boost their preposterous claim to Partition which is being paid for by British lives.

"If it should be conclusively proved that the murder was committed by Eoka I shall at once express my regret for an erroneous belief. Meanwhile, I retain that belief, though I shall never assert that it *was* committed by a Turk without further evidence."

Tory M.P.s in marginal seats were writing to the B.B.C. to complain that some of the constituents were asking why the B.B.C. were going to produce a television series with somebody who seemed on terms with the bloodthirsty Makarios.

"I do not believe that all the constituents of some M.P.s are as stupid as their M.P. himself, but if you think that I have become too unpopular a figure to appear on television let me come on in *What's Your Line* and if the studio audience hisses like an angry flock of geese you can hold up *The Glory that was Greece* until the Government comes to its senses about Cyprus. And if you have a *This is Your Life* in view in which I could take part that's another way of testing an audience's reaction."

As I looked at the team sitting blindfold on either side of Eamonn Andrews to guess who was the unknown 'well-known' I was more successful in disguising my voice than I had been on two previous occasions. Indeed, I had the team so flummoxed that Eamonn had to come to their rescue and by dropping a hint gave Lady Barnett a clue which she at once solved. The audience gave a round of applause and nobody by hissing suggested that she had unmasked Public Enemy Number One.

The anxiety of the B.B.C. about my shaking hands with Makarios was allayed, but I agreed to take part in *This is Your Life* of which Bransby Williams was to be the subject at the beginning of that December.

Bransby Williams in 1958 was a year older than I am as I write these words, and it was all but fifty years since to please my father I had agreed to play in Hall Caine's play *The Bishop's Son* which ran for only a week at the Garrick Theatre in 1910.

I was touched to receive this letter from that gallant old pro:

My very dear Friend,
I can't find words to say how proud and touched I was when you walked in on me—it was a most emotional surprise to me. Oh, the memories and all dear friends surrounding me at the end and then our happy drink and sandwiches.
Well God bless you old friend.

Yours ever
Bransby.

Bransby Williams was having a difficult time in his old age, and it was decided to celebrate his 89th birthday with a testimonial cheque with which it was hoped to give him some well earned comfort in his old age.

Lord Birkett was the Chairman and the Patrons were Emlyn Williams, Lord Brabazon, John Gielgud, Donald Wolfit, Beverley Baxter and myself. It is good to be able to remember that the testimonial was a success and that it was possible to help somebody who for seventy years had been entertaining the public all over the world.

The rest of that December was spent finishing off the job begun in Greece. Filming was to start at the Ealing Studios on December 1st and I had ten days in which to prepare my commentary in vision.

It had been the intention of the producer that I should address the viewer directly at important places like the beach at Marathon or the mound at Thermopylae. To speak in vision requires a synchronised camera in which film stock and sound stock should run at exactly the same speed so that the lip movements tally with the speaker's words. This cannot be done with an ordinary 35-mm silent camera, though silent cameras which can be adapted to sound use do exist. Therefore in order to do the 'direct to camera' sequences an alternative to a sound camera was required unless extra technicians and a great deal more equipment had been taken to Greece. That would have doubled the cost of filming besides complicating the problem of transport. So it was decided to use Back Projection.

Back Projection is a technique used in films to avoid exposing the actors to danger or to publicity in places like Piccadilly Circus. The scene is shot without sound and the film is projected on a large screen in a studio, the actors being placed in front of that screen. Their performance is then filmed by a sound camera. All car chases are made that way if they involve dialogue by the stern hero (or gangster) and the anxious heroine (or gangster's moll). They sit in a static car while behind them is run a film of the road from a moving car.

There was a little anxiety at Lime Grove whether a documentary film should be allowed to deceive viewers into thinking that I was actually on the beach at Marathon when they heard me talking about it as if I was still there. The answer to that was that I did go to every place shown on the screen and did say with a tape-recorder

more or less what I should be saying at Ealing. The use of Back
Projection was merely a technical convenience to save expense and
additional equipment.

As it was, to load five mules with delicate film equipment and
scramble up that boulder-strewn mountain path to the Dictaean
Cave was taking quite enough risks. If anything had gone wrong
with the gear at the beginning of our shooting in Crete we might
have been unable to complete the programme in time.

So a special Back Projection camera was brought to Greece. This
is an ordinary silent camera but of a much heavier make, so that the
picture when it appears on a large screen will not jig about. I
would appear, move out of vision at the cue, and then the camera
would film four or five minutes of the background from which I
had moved. When possible there was movement in that background.
At the Dictaean Cave my mule went on swishing its tail; tourists
would wander round at Knossos and Thermopylae, the tourists
being Stephen Hearst, Paddy Leigh Fermor, Milto Spyromilios and
Chrissie; a bus drove just behind me by the Mound at Marathon;
the motion of the ferry-boat at Salamis was reproduced; if my hair
was blowing in vision an artificial draught blew it about in the
studio. Sometimes I was shot walking from right to left, sometimes
from left to right, so that when I appeared against the large screen
at Ealing I was apparently continuing the walk I had been taking
a month or two before. Continuity had to be carefully watched. If
I was carrying my hat in my left hand and my stick in my right hand
as I descended the Mound at Marathon I had to arrive in front
of that Mound in Ealing with hat and stick in the same hands and
wearing the same suit and tie.

It was Chrissie's job to keep notes of those appearances in Greece:

B.P. No. 5.

*No waistcoat. Spectacle case in pocket. No hat. Green spotted tie. Green
shirt. Green socks. Brogues not the brown buckskin shoes. No stick.*

There is a variety of technical tricks to make studio scenes convincing. Studio sound differs from natural sound as shot on location.
When I was standing on the deck of a ferry-boat in Salamis Bay
my voice had to contend with the sound of a motor and the splashing
of the waves against the sides. In the silence of the studio some of
these sounds had to be reproduced without making me raise my
voice.

This method of filming in the studio saves much worry if one goes to remote places and wants to record sound sequences, but it imposes a considerable strain on the performer, the director and the crew. No speaker who is not a natural actor should ever be asked to do any sequences which involve Back Projection. The performer, surrounded by about twenty technicians in the glaring light of studio arcs, is standing in front of a screen and talking to a lens and at the same time imagining that he is still standing under the azure sky of Greece. If he has not been able to transport himself back in fancy the ruthless medium of television will communicate his failure to an audience of alarming perspicacity. The performer has to remember that the film running behind him on the screen will last only as long as the original amount shot in Greece. Therefore what he has to say must be said within at most five minutes or he will be talking in front of a blank screen. It is of course absolutely essential that the cameraman who shot the original sequence should do the studio sequences as well, because he alone knows the intensity of light he allowed for in Greece (or wherever else this method be used) and that must be matched with the studio lighting, a highly skilled operation.

We had five days in which to do the Back Projection of the three films, working for a full eight hours a day, and by December 5th we were all very tired. I had written out what I intended to say in vision and I contemplated learning this by heart. On consideration I was afraid that the strain on my memory might lead me to concentrate on that instead of upon holding my audience. So I decided to content myself with knowing the substance of what I had to say and speaking extempore. Inevitably, once or twice, I would stumble or omit something of vital importance and they would have to restart the screen film, but everybody in the studio managed to make me feel that it was really a treat for them to hear me explaining the Athenian Constitution all over again, and I was able to respond once or twice by giving an impression that I enjoyed doing it all over again when it was the camera that misbehaved instead of myself.

Almost at the end on the last day I made an idiotic mistake at the second time of showing the potsherd on which the name of Themistocles had been scratched for ostracism. For the first time in my life I pronounced it as 'pots-herd' instead of 'pot-sherd'. I knew I had done this but by this time I was so tired and everybody else was so tired that I could not bring myself to do the bit again and I decided to take a chance that nobody would notice the solecism.

In fact only one viewer did write me a reproachful letter and I hope my humble apology satisfied him.

After the Back Projection ordeal was over I had a very busy few days in London including a report to the Cyprus Reconciliation Committee in the House of Commons, to which Sir Harold Nicolson and I were co-opted from outside when it was formed. I also took the chair as Honorary President of the National Cypriot Organisation at a great meeting in the Royal Hotel, Bloomsbury, where I was able to say what I had been unable to say in Athens. On my way out from the meeting an ex-Indian Army Colonel spoke to me with approval of my speech. This gave me particular pleasure because, as one of those who had shown the world what the British imperial mission could be at its best, he knew what he was talking about. The pride, respect, and affection with which India and Pakistan look back on that old Indian Army is the noblest monument of all to the British Empire.

But Back Projection was not yet over. I was rung up to hear that the beach of Marathon had misbehaved itself by jumping about behind me and that the back projection of my looking down from the Acropolis at the Agora of Athens and then giving my account of the Athenian Constitution would have to be done standing instead of sitting. So could I come back from Scotland next week and do it again? The studio was not available till then. I protested against having to come down before Christmas and finally it was arranged that the studio should be available for an evening. Encased in wool under my summer suit I braved the chill December air, stood again upon the beach at Marathon and on the Acropolis made my remarks about the Athenian Constitution upright instead of sitting.

While I worked in Edinburgh upon the commentary out of vision, Stephen, Charles and Johnny were working hard down in London. Each shot of a hoplite came from a photograph of a Greek vase which had to be filmed. Each shot of a Persian warrior came from photographs of the famous reliefs at Persepolis and these had to be filmed. Greek triremes were filmed from vases in the British museum, Phoenician ships from Sidonian coins not so big as a halfpenny. These had to be photographed, enlarged, and then filmed with a 'tracking shot' to give movement. Maps and titles had to be drawn and filmed. The editor and the producer were sifting and selecting to give rhythm and flow to the whole. A shot held a second too long, an abrupt 'cut' from shot to unrelated shot,

C.M. with Cretan peasants, 1958

Chrissie, C.M., Milto Spyromilo, Johnny Ray and Stephen Hearst

The Archbishop Makarios and C.M.

C.M. and Lord Boothby

two consecutive camera movements in opposite directions—all these can worry the viewer without his being able to say why. Eventually the film is cut and the music 'laid' on its own separate track. The length of each shot is then measured and described on a short list. Only when the final length of each individual shot is known can the commentary be written in exactly the number of words required.

H

I CAME to London at the end of January to finish off my part
of *The Glory that was Greece* by dubbing the commentary, and I
found those three days at Ealing and Alexandra Palace the most
difficult of all. I sat in what is not much larger than a packing-case
with a glass front. Beside me was Jean Dumbleton, Stephen Hearst's
secretary, whose job it was to prod me gently when I had to begin
reading. The film as cut was run off on a screen at the other end of
the little theatre beyond the very warm and tiny conservatory in
which Jean and I were sitting. With earphones I could listen to what
I was saying in vision. As the film ran, numbers succeeded numbers
beside the film at the rate of one a second. My cue to begin reading
would perhaps be 142. I would take the earphones off about twenty
seconds before this and rely on Jean's prod for my cue. While I
was reading of course I could not watch the pictures running by.
When the forty seconds of film was finished Stephen would give the
verdict. 'Five seconds late on the profile of Zeus'. 'Nine seconds late
for the head of Themistocles'. It was vital for me to say 'Themistocles' in my commentary at the exact second when the bust of him
appeared on the screen.

So the words would be cut here and there, which was not an easy
job because my commentary had already been cut to the bone. It
may be asked why I could not pick up the necessary seconds by
quickening the rate of reading. The answer is that the reading out
of vision must be at the same pitch and the same tempo as the
numbers in vision which often carried on directly into the dubbed
commentary.

By the time I had watched each film run through three or four
times I was so sick of the sound of my own voice and the sight of my
own face that I began to have grave doubts about the success of the
whole series. Moreover, my voice in that January weather seemed
to me sounding tired by the end of the exhausting day, and I felt
that the reassurances of Stephen were a kindly evasion of the truth.

"The dubbing mixer says it's all right now," I was told.

The dubbing mixer controls all sound levels and his is an intricate
job demanding extreme technical accomplishment. The film finally

runs with the commentary on one sound track, the music on another, and effects such as thunder, drums, or footsteps on a third.

By February 15, 1959, the three films were ready for the final laboratory processing, and the first of them was offered to viewers on April 1st. The critics of the Press were unanimously generous to the final product, and what gave me particular pleasure was the recognition that Stephen Hearst and Charles de Jaeger received for the remarkable job they had done.

I hope that I have been able to give the public some idea of what goes on behind the scenes before a series like *The Glory that was Greece* appears on television sets all over the country, but I feel that I may have made it sound easier than it is, at any rate for the producer on whose shoulders rests by far the heaviest weight of responsibility.

The many letters I received from viewers included three from octogenarians and over a dozen from teenagers, and I was delighted to read in a Liverpool paper that there had been a run on books about Greece in the municipal children's library in Liverpool, due— the librarian thought—to the television series called *The Glory that was Greece*. So much for those who say that television is keeping children from reading. That will happen with the next generation, technologically educated in an attempt to compete with Russia and ultimately with China. I do wish that both the B.B.C. and I.T.V. would plan their television for schools as an entertainment in the way of education. It is no use thinking that a dull exponent of history in the classroom will be any less dull on a television set; indeed, in television, as in after-dinner speeches, manner is as important as matter.

A technological education of the young at the expense of classics and history will benefit only Communism. If I had learned Russian and German in my youth instead of Greek and Latin I am sure I should be a passionate Communist in my old age. Guided minds are much more powerful than guided missiles, but misguided minds are not less powerful.

I ask myself now ten years later whether I could write with equal optimism about the effect of television on children's reading, or for that matter on reading at any age. I fancy that by the end of the 21st century the man who can read will be regarded with the respect that today we accord to a Sanskrit scholar. However, I console myself for that gloomy fancy by hoping that women will still be able to read.

Mercifully children are still able to respond to the past, however many of them respond to the adventures in outer space on television in which wherever the gallant astronauts go they find that the inhabitants of space speak the same Greater London English as themselves with just as many 'Y'knows'.

I was to enjoy a heartening experience some years later. I quote from the prologue to my book about Herakles called *The Strongest Man on Earth*:

"In the month of March 1966 I was one of the people who tell stories to small boys and girls in a B.B.C. series called *Jackanory*. I chose for the stories I would tell the adventures of two heroes of ancient Greece called Perseus and Theseus. I had no idea whether I should be able to make those adventures interesting to the children of today, although when I was eight years old I had been fascinated by a book called *The Heroes*, written by Charles Kingsley. To my delight and a good deal to my surprise I had a lot of letters from five-year-olds, six-year-olds, seven-year-olds, eight-year-olds, nine-year-olds, ten-year-olds and even one or two from twelve-year-olds, asking for more stories about that wonderful land of ancient Greece. So I made up my mind I would try to tell some more stories of that beautiful country, and put them in a book."

I quote now from the Epilogue:

"You may have thought sometimes when you were reading the story of Herakles that his exploits were not unlike those of Samson, and I want you to realise that Herakles was as much a real human being once upon a time as Samson.

"The stories that people tell about us three thousand years hence will seem just as improbable as some of the stories we are told about people three thousand years ago. They will find it hard to believe that once upon a time great nations were planning to obliterate each other with atom bombs.

"When we read about dragons and flying horses and gigantic serpents we must remember that those memories were kept alive by tales handed down of prehistoric monsters when human beings really did have to preserve themselves from dinosaurs and pterodactyls. When we read about the Nemean lion we must remember that in the dim and distant past a sabre-toothed tiger might make the neighbourhood extremely dangerous for people armed only with stones.

"When boys and girls three thousand years hence read about Hitler they will wonder if such an evil monster like that could ever have really existed. Yet we know that he *did* exist.

"I first read about those heroes of ancient Greece nearly eighty years ago and I am as much enthralled by their adventures now as I was when I first read about them."

Faith became 81 in this February and I was becoming more and more worried about what I realised was the failure of the Drummond Place flat to make her old age happy. And then Nicolas Nadegine died. For fifty years that figure from a play or story by Chekhov had been associated with us. He was almost a great barytone and star of Italian opera. The gramophone records of his voice were almost best sellers. The volume of poems dedicated to Faith and me was almost recognised as the promise of another Pushkin. His marriage to an Australian girl might have been a success if she had not fallen in love with Kerensky and obtained a divorce to marry him. I could chronicle more 'almosts' of 'Bim' as he was nicknamed. With a bass singer who was nicknamed 'Boom' he came to Capri after the Bolsheviks had put the Mensheviks out of the Russian Embassy in Rome.

For Faith the death of Nadegine was as if the three volumes of her autobiography *As Much as I Dare*, *More than I should* and *Always Afternoon* had been destroyed. She began to pine again for Sheffield Terrace, and finally she went to a nursing home in Brunswick Gardens close by. Ann Asher was her devoted companion for a while and later Nellie Eastwood took on this duty.

The success that *The Glory that was Greece* had was some reward for Mrs Wyndham Goldie, without whose support of my original suggestion and without whose choice of Stephen Hearst as the ideal producer *The Glory that was Greece* would never have been televised.

Of the many letters I received none gave me greater pleasure than one from Tamara Talbot Rice. She really did know Greece:

We listened to you last week entranced and fascinated. I thought of writing to tell you how grateful we were for your so evocative a talk, then—thinking of your fan mail and fearing to add to it—I desisted. Instead we and our friends here talked to each other of the pleasure you had given us. George Spencer Churchill of Northwick and the Ustinovs—Peter's parents—were amongst the most appreciative. And now tonight, you have given us so much further pleasure and delight that, even at the risk of adding to your mail, I feel that I must write both to thank you for two half hours of enchantment, and to congratulate you on a truly masterly achievement. And since I neither expect nor indeed want you to waste time in answering this note, I hope you won't mind my sending it.

*We leave for Trebizond at the end of the month to spend several weeks
uncovering some Byzantine art in the Cathedral of St Sophia there. We look
forward to seeing you on our return.*

I was surprised and deeply moved to receive a letter from the
Queen of the Hellenes who was staying incognita at Claridges. In
this, Queen Frederika's lady-in-waiting told me that by chance her
Majesty had turned on the television to hear the last film of *The
Glory that was Greece* and had been carried unexpectedly back to
Greece.

In May it was decided that Lily who had tackled the job of
becoming a professional hairdresser with much zeal should have a
holiday in Italy before our hairdressing salon was to be opened this
autumn.

I had to go down to London a night before her. Carol Costello
offered to drive me to the Waverley Station and Lily came along
too for any last words I might have about our journey to Rome.
We were sitting in my sleeping compartment when suddenly the
train started to move out of the station and would not stop until it
reached Newcastle.

We asked the sleeping-car attendant if he could call for the guard.
When he was asked if the train could be stopped at the next station
he shook his head.

"But I have a baby boy at home all alone and I cannot leave him
alone all night."

Some note of despair in Carol's voice touched the guard's heart.

"Well, I'll do my best," he said, "I'll drop a piece of paper out
asking them to ring Longniddry and signal the train to stop there
for half a minute."

"But couldn't you tell the driver to do that?" I asked.

"I'm not in communication with the driver," he replied.

"Do you mean to say that whatever happens on the train you
cannot communicate with the driver?"

"Only by pulling the communication cord."

I do not know if this is still the only way in which a guard can
communicate with the driver of his train. However, it would not
surprise me to hear an affirmative. Nothing surprises me about
British Railways not even when a train arrives dead on time.

Fortunately the note the guard dropped at the station before
Longniddry was picked up, and at Longniddry the train pulled up
for Carol and Lily to scramble out on an unlighted platform, from

which in the darkness they set out to find out if there was any means of transport back to Edinburgh available. To their relief the last bus, mercifully behind time, was going to Edinburgh and about two in the morning Lily got back to Drummond Place to prepare for catching her train to London at ten that morning.

We did not fly to Rome. I never fly unless it is absolutely necessary. I think that one of the reasons for the muddle the world is in is the habit of statesmen, politicians and civil servants arriving in places before their brains.

It was heartwarming to find the P.L.M. station in Paris almost unchanged. Even the train for Rome left at the same minute after eight as it had before the First War.

Alas, the long loop round Rome was sadly different. Hardly a glimpse of the campagna now and only concrete ant-heap after ant-heap of flats met the eye. 'This morn of Rome and May' of which Browning sang could no longer inspire a poet. It was hard to believe amid the surge and noise of the motor traffic that once upon a time one had driven down the Esquiline in a clip-clopping carozza past strollers who did not bother to keep to the pavement.

Of course I had realised the change in Rome when I was there in 1947, but on this visit a decade later I was back in an Italy of over forty years ago when Rome was the quietest city in Europe.

Delia and Jack Lennie had moved from Edinburgh to Rome only about a month before Lily and I arrived but Delia had found rooms for us in a comfortable hotel, the Hotel Ludovisi in Via Ludovisi, off the Via Veneto. I was glad to find what a tonic effect Rome was having on Jack Lennie. He was already *Romano di Roma*. Paul was already at school and Nadina was to go to school in the autumn.

While we were sitting outside one of the cafés in the Via Veneto drinking our pre-lunch Campari at least a dozen British tourists alighting from various busloads recognised me and after telling me how much they had enjoyed *The Glory that was Greece* went on to suppose that I would presently be doing *The Grandeur that was Rome*. As I had managed to ascend those back-breaking steps to the top of the Colosseum I did not feel at all daunted by the grandeur of Rome. However, when I got back to England and perhaps a little complacently told the B.B.C. of this encouraging behaviour of viewers I was told that Sir Mortimer Wheeler was going to proclaim the grandeur of Rome.

I returned to my efforts to persuade the B.B.C. to do six half-hour films about the life of Robert Louis Stevenson, starting in Edinburgh and finishing beside his tomb in Samoa. I pointed out that the reason why the B.B.C. had failed to get *The Glory that was Greece* taken into the United States was that the three programmes were each forty minutes long which was the wrong length for commercial television. I argued that *The Glory that was Greece* had had a great success in Australia, New Zealand, South Africa and Canada and that R.L.S. might be a still greater success.

Roy and Elizabeth Munro arrived in Rome to stay in the Hotel Ludovisi and we had many drives together. I recall looking down at Lake Nemi, as exquisite a view as any in Italy. Mussolini had caused Lake Nemi to be drained in order to recover a Roman galleon believed to be at the bottom and full of gold. The galleon was recovered but the gold—it was found to be one more myth. We visited the Forum by moonlight which I had never managed to do on earlier visits to Rome. We went to Ostia Antica which was once the port of Rome but was now twenty miles inland. Here a millennium and a half was but yesterday when we saw the ruts made by Roman chariots and the inn at which St Augustine and his mother St Monica stayed on the night before he left Rome for Africa.

Then Roy and Elizabeth left to drive back home in their new green Jaguar. They had a remarkable youngest son called Dougal who at the age of seven used to visit me at Drummond Place where we discussed life together. I am glad to think that as I write about this seven-year-old he is now in his last term at Glenalmond and Captain of that famous school.

After the Munros left Rome Jack Lennie drove us up to Fiesole where we stayed at the Villa La Scalette, the beautiful villa belonging to Delia Lennie's younger sister Nadia Conenna. Florence was not so noisy as Rome but like Rome it was suffering from the tyranny of the motor-car. The Devil's most distinguished exploit in the way of mischief has always been considered his temptation of Eve and Adam's feeble and typically masculine excuses for his own behaviour. I think that his most mischievous exploit was his gift to man of the internal combustion engine. Motor-cars, aeroplanes, the atom bomb, and who knows what horrors may come in the future from humanity's enslavement to machinery. The added comforts for the human body do not compensate for the ever growing discomfort of the human mind.

I wrote to tell Faith not to be too sad because she was no longer able to visit her beloved Florence.

I had never seen Pisa and we had the pleasure of doing this with Jack Lennie. So often places are so familiar in pictures that when one sees them at last they are somehow disappointing, looking exactly like what one expected them to look. I recall my failure to be awed by Niagara and what seemed to me the dullness of the Pyramids. The leaning tower of Pisa was familiar enough in photographs. Nevertheless, when we sat in its shadow and I gazed up at that architectural eccentricity I found it as much more surprising as, in a grander way, I found my first sight of the Acropolis.

We also stopped at Sienna for an hour to refresh ourselves. As we sat looking across that great cobbled *piazza* I was back five centuries and well able to understand how the Siennese were able to sustain their annual display of medieval pageantry as naturally as if the costumes they wore were the costumes of their everyday life.

We were sad to leave Rome but so many past days in Rome came back almost wistfully when Cook's made the usual muddle they always used to make over our wagon-lit. At Victoria Lily was very indignant when she was charged £2 10s for a leather handbag she had bought in Rome but her indignation was mollified by the failure of the Customs officer to notice that the woollen coat over her arm had also been bought in Rome.

I was sad to get a letter from Bill Hutchison[1] to say he and Margery were leaving Edinburgh:

3 Cheniston Gardens Studios,
Kensington, W.8.

My dear Monty,

Margery and I have closed 11 Eglinton Crescent and are now at this address, (very hot it is, too, today), but we have also bought a house at Richmond on the river. It is a Queen Anne Building, and only suffers from flooding at high tide, otherwise it is in our sight, quite perfect. We hope to be in before Christmas.

But I am really writing to say that coming South by the 4 o'clock train, the other day, feeling pretty worn and tired with packing etc., and looking for something to read at Waverley my eye rested on a Penguin I hadn't seen before —'Water on the Brain'. What a lucky chance, what a delight, what a gem! I spent the pleasantest journey thinking I heard your voice telling me of B and P and N of the Darling Renatu and all the rest, suppressing my chuckles as best I could, and enjoying every turn in the wonderful complications.

I have now passed it to M who is as enthusiastic as I am. We shall be in Edinburgh in August and hope to see you then.

Meantime our love to you and yours.

Bill.

[1] The late Sir William Hutchison.

It was not surprising that the former President of the Royal Scottish Academy was leaving that beautiful studio. He was so busy in London with one portrait after another that Edinburgh was becoming merely an occasional interruption of his life in London. I had last enjoyed the company of Bill and Margery on that Aegean cruise I had taken in 1957. Bill had done a portrait of me in Eglinton Crescent but Margery had decided that it was not good enough and made him destroy it.

I had been very pleased when Dent's decided to publish a third edition of my children's book *Santa Claus in Summer* which had been originally published by Constable's in 1924 and perfectly illustrated by 'Neenie' Watson as she then was. A second edition was published in the 'thirties by Blackwell but Neenie Macdonald's (as she had become) illustrations were not used. To my relief Dent's agreed to use the original illustrations. For this third edition (still in print I am happy to say) Neenie Macdonald had done what I think is the most attractive jacket for a children's book I have ever seen. I was grateful to her for the work she did on that jacket because at the time, already a widow herself, she was nursing a dearly loved sister who was dying.

I was not too hopeful about the success of the nursing home in Brunswick Gardens. However, I realised that no matter where Faith was she would find her surroundings an intrusion upon the past in which she was beginning to live. I was nevertheless cheered to hear that she was contemplating a book about Majorca which was at any rate an experience of the more recent past. She seemed to have put the book she had planned to write about Lucca out of mind altogether. One of the troubles was her inability to concentrate on the radio. I find a letter telling her that I was sorry she had not heard my talk about the Kaiser and that Prince Frederick of Prussia had written to thank me for the sympathetic portrait of him.

In the same letter I was telling of my effort to get *Cats in my Life* finished in time for Christmas publication. Why I changed the title to *Cats' Company* I cannot now think. Perhaps it was because I was also writing *Greece in my Life* and the publishers wanted me to change. In the end I was to find that in choosing *Cats' Company* I had used the title of Michael Joseph's delightful book *Cat's Company*. All I could do was apologise with profound regret to Mrs Michael Joseph who was good enough to accept that apology in the kindest way. Several of my books have provided titles for other people. Some third rate thriller writer called one of his productions *Sinister Street*.

Matheson Lang used *Carnival* for a play translated from the Italian with another title although a dramatisation of *Carnival* had already been produced. The *Evening Standard* ran my novel *Fairy Gold* as a serial and a few years later published another serial called *Fairy Gold!*. The note of exclamation seems a justifiable exclamation of surprise. *Thin Ice* was used for some skating manual. *The Darkening Green* was used inadvertently and the author wrote a charming letter of apology. A day or two ago in 1970 I read the announcement of some play or TV series that was to be called *April Fools*.

There is no copyright in titles provided the book is not a deliberate imitation of its predecessor. Obviously such a copyright would be impossible to administer.

Cats' Company which I still think should have been called *Cats in my Life* had a success and I have received nearly two hundred letters about it from all over the world. I am hoping one day to publish selections from these which I shall call *Mews of the World*. I had originally thought of calling such a selection *Whiskers Galore* but I doubt if the average assistant at all but the few bookshops still intelligently managed today would recognise the difference between *Whisky* and *Whiskers*.

For me the number of good books about cats being published both in Great Britain and the United States is an encouragement to hope that individuals will be able to exist even when most of their fellows have surrendered to the herd.

I should feel much more optimistic about a Prime Minister's ability to lead his country if he were a cat lover rather than a dog lover. Dogs lead a man to suppose that he is more able than in fact he is, and also that he is better loved than in fact he is. It is to be noted that we speak of a dog's master; we never allude to a cat's master.

Early in October I received a letter from the wife of Quartermaster-Sergeant —— stationed in Edinburgh—a letter which deeply impressed me:

Dear Sir,

I am an admirer of my husband who in turn is an admirer of you.

My husband is in the regular army. Sgt. R.A.S.C. stationed at Edinburgh Castle. He is an Englishman born in Burgess Hill in Sussex.

I am sure you must be thinking "the woman's daft writing to tell me about her husband" but there is method in my madness.

Every time my husband sees you on Television or sees your photo in the papers he says "now there is a man I would really like to meet."

Well, as I told you at the beginning I admire my husband and I would like him to meet you. I have never requested anything like this in my life before and for all I know a yellow van might draw up at my door and whisk me away to the nearest mental home.

The way I look at it though is that although you are from a different class to us we are all God's children and I might be allowed to put this request to you.

Our home is a humble one though the army might not like to hear me say this as it's made up of army furniture, in fact everything is army apart from my children and animals, but I would like you very much to come here one evening to meet my husband.

On reading through this letter it sounds like awful cheek but nothing dared, nothing achieved. My husband knows nothing of this letter so far and I shall await a reply before telling him what I have done.

Yours faithfully,

Jean ——

I wrote to say how much I should enjoy a visit and Mrs F—— wrote on October 9th:

My husband and I have great pleasure in accepting your invitation to meet you on Tuesday next at 9 p.m.

I hinted to my husband what I had done but when your so prompt reply came I was so amazed I just let him read it for himself. I don't think the shock could have been so great if I told him he'd scooped the pools.

My mother is in Edinburgh so I will have no trouble in finding a baby-sitter and look forward eagerly to Tuesday evening.

Yours sincerely,

Jean F——

After the visit Mrs F—— wrote me another letter, and I was glad to know they had enjoyed the evening as much as I had:

A note of thanks for a lovely evening. I don't know who was more thrilled— my husband or my son (with his autograph book). I was most certainly over-whelmed by the kindness and interest shown to us by everyone.

Towards the end of the evening I just couldn't speak, the first time (my husband said) that I have ever been stuck for words.

I don't think I shall ever forget the evening we spent with you and to make quite sure I don't, Compton is going to be among my next baby's names (I'm sure it's a boy) then I shall be able to tell him that about four weeks before his birth I sat in your house talking to you.

I have spent about an hour over this letter because I just can't find words to tell you how much we appreciated your kindness to us. Our grateful thanks to everyone for making us feel so at home.

This was the beginning of a friendship I much enjoyed and when the Quartermaster-Sergeant was ordered to Hong Kong we corresponded at intervals. I was delighted to hear in 1968 that he was coming back to Great Britain, but to my sorrow he died suddenly after settling down in Ireland to which he was posted and I never saw that splendid fellow again.

The memory of that friendship with the F—— revives my faith in the ultimate ability of democracy to fulfil the Divine purpose.

I find a photograph on the back of which is written:

From Charles F—— aged 9 to Sir Compton Mackenzie whose autograph I shall always cherish.

Charles F—— must be 20 as I write these words, and I hope that I shall see him again and be reminded of his remarkable father.

Vyvyan Holland was feeling less optimistic about democracy than I was that October. He was writing from 12 Grosvenor Court:

"I note, from my morning paper today, that you have called the Tories 'a lot of boneheads'. Why pick on the Tories particularly? Surely, *all* politicians are boneheads? Otherwise they would not be politicians. I am a Liberal myself—that is to say, I have no particular political creed except that most politicians are scoundrels, and the majority of them are only out for what they can get for themselves and don't really care one hoot in Hell for the countries of which they are, were, or would like to be Dictators.

Best wishes as always,
from Vyvyan"

I had supposed that the reason why my novel *Water on the Brain* has never been filmed or televised was the desire by Intelligence, whether M.I.5 or M.I.6, to avoid being laughed at by a much larger audience than any book attracts. A letter I received from a doctor in San Francisco suggested that *Water on the Brain* might have been considered a threat to the secrecy of our secret service. The book had been translated both into French and German and that may have worried our secret service. That letter from San Francisco made me realise what a threat *Water on the Brain* must have seemed and how lucky I was not to have been prosecuted again under the Official Secrets Act:

"Your 'New Preface' to 'Water on the Brain' which I saw for the first time in the Penguin edition impels me to let you know that your book *was* used as a text in a U.S. Intelligence agency, O.S.S. Since copies were not procurable in 1942, one hundred photocopies were made.

"There is one special peculiarity of this great book—when it is loaned, it is never returned; when it is placed in an open bookshelf, it is stolen. At various times I have had several copies of the 1933 edition. I have been able to keep one. Fortunately the Penguin edition will relieve the pressure."

I thought for a moment that my correspondent must be playing a joke on my credulity but a second reading convinced me that I was being told the simple truth. The very next day came a letter from Cleveland, Ohio telling me the same story. That letter I have lost but a few months later came a letter from a Radio and Television station in New York State:

"Back during World War II, you may have known that the American Office of Strategic Services circulated the book to its many agents in the hopes that appropriate lessons would be learned by those smart enough to learn. There weren't any copies of the book available. Having a monstrous secret budget, the O.S.S. copied the book by typewriter, and then reproduced it photographically in a few copies. These were a kind of required reading during the training and indoctrination period."

People are so much addicted to thrillers that they are becoming almost affectionate towards 'spies' who were released in 1970 after serving a term of imprisonment for selling naval information to a foreign power. They were at once interviewed on television and presented to the public as two sweethearts separated for 9 years instead of the petty traitors they were. At the same time an elderly M.P. who had been prosecuted under the Official Secrets Act for allegedly revealing to a Czechoslovak Press Attaché the proceedings of some House of Commons Committee was presented as a blackmailed innocent, for whom the public should be sentimentally sorry. House of Commons secrets have always been Punch's secrets and to suppose that any of them could have been useful to a foreign power is as improbable as the adventures of James Bond. Nevertheless, it was the blackmailed not the blackmailer who took the money.

On October 31st, 1959, Lilian's hairdressing salon in the basement of 31 Drummond Place was opened by Andrew Strachan with whom Lily had been working since she finished her training in London at Morris's school of hairdressing and Mrs Gertrude Hartley's School of beauty-culture. This generous gesture by Andrew Strachan was a recognition of Lily's competence and a salute to the loyal service she had given to himself. Mrs Helena Kean, a delightful Belgian, who had managed the women's hairdressing department of the Caledonian Hotel until it was given up, joined Lilian's and is still there in 1970.

I wrote to Faith:

"I've had to write half a dozen tiresome articles, and so unable to get on with my cat book. The salon is doing quite well, the wages being covered in the first week. We are lucky having a very good number 2 for Lily.

"The weather is frightful! And I've no doubt it is equally frightful in London. In my mail this morning a letter from New Zealand to tell me that the Maoris are one of the Lost Tribes and that Winston Churchill's great great grandmother was an Iroquois squaw; a letter from Portugal addressed to the Rt. Hon. Sir Compton Mackenzie, President of the National Cat Club, England to ask for my bookplate, and a request from a Congregational minister to pay £10 towards his daughter's education."

Whether Winston Churchill did have a Red Indian ancestress I do not know, but I feel sure that I had one and have always attributed to that remote ancestress my ability to fight pain and ignore anxiety. I have never lost half-an-hour's sleep from worrying.

Evelyn Waugh had been up in Edinburgh some months previously to talk to Winifred Peck[1] the sister of Ronnie Knox[2] whose life he was writing. We had had a long talk. I recall his telling me that he did not think he should be able to complete his trilogy of novels about the war and my saying such doubts were those of every genuinely creative writer as he approaches sixty. I had just read Evelyn's life of Ronnie Knox and had written to congratulate him upon the wonderful way in which he had been able to present the Oxford of Ronnie Knox's times.

On November 17th he wrote to me from Combe Florey House, Nr. Taunton:

I think perhaps you can imagine how much your letter exhilarated me. Praise from you at any time is something to horde—no hoard—rejoicing. Praise

---

[1] Lady Peck.   [2] The Rt. Rev. Mgr. Ronald Knox.

for my Life of Ronnie, which touches your own experience at so many points, is a unique satisfaction. It is most generous of you not to resent the intrusion of a younger man into places he barely knows. Thank you very much indeed for going to the trouble to write. It would have been so easy to have said with the best will, 'I'll say a word to him when we next meet.' But alas, we don't meet much, do we? I have greedy memories of dining with you in Edinburgh. Someone told me a barber had opened shop in your beautiful home, surely not?

You, I take it, are hibernating. I toil with a pot-boiler and then bolt to the Mediterranean. I never spend a night in London that I can avoid. You did say you might be coming to Magdalen one day. Don't please forget we are directly on the way.

I had seen more of Alec Waugh who was a member of the Savile than of Evelyn who was a member of White's, but whenever we did meet was an occasion to remember with warmth. I never saw a sign of rising bristles and the only time I think I gave him a momentary shock was when I said I thought that another Catholic author was a Jansenist at heart.

When I had last been in London I had lunched with somebody of the *Daily Express* and said the Gambols were the best of all the strip cartoons, and that it was the Gambols who kept me faithful to the *Daily Express*. He seemed surprised by this and when I got back to Edinburgh I felt I must testify to that strip cartoon. Barry Appleby wrote:

"It was a delight to receive your letter and to know that you enjoy The Gambols cartoon. Coming from a Master Strip Writer this is indeed praise of the highest order."

How glad I am to be able to testify over ten years later to the astonishing endurance of the Gambols. It evidently gave pleasure that some one who had had an association however brief with Flook knew what it meant to compose a strip cartoon.

I had another letter that week from somebody else who is still going strong. That was from Fanny Craddock of the Bon Viveur at Shooters Hill asking me if I could come to dinner next month and officially declare their new "dream kitchen" open. Ten years later Fanny Cradock is still the fairy godmother of a dream kitchen for the B.B.C.

One more letter I received toward the end of that year is for me a less jolly memory. Gilbert Harding wrote:

"*Dearest Monty,*

The post office charged me fourpence to receive your letter dated November 25th (perhaps that's why it came only on Friday after-noon).

"I will join the Society of St Augustine right away.

"It was delightful and delicious, delirious and d'lovely to see you looking so young and so vigorous at the Club.

Ever affectionately
Gilbert"

Almost exactly a year later I was down in London for two or three days and was expecting to see Gilbert Harding at the Savile. On the third evening after my arrival as I got out of the taxi Gilbert was emerging from 69 Brook Street. It was about half past six in the evening.

"For goodness sake," I exclaimed, "do come back in again for a short gossip. You've not been near the Club since I came down from Edinburgh."

"I can't, my dear friend," he said. I forget what his appointment was. Then just before he stepped into the taxi in which I had arrived he put his two hands on my shoulders and kissed me on each cheek.

"Goodbye, Monty, goodbye."

Three hours later he was dead.

I was asked to take part in the tribute to him by the B.B.C. I cannot find the text of what I said but I am under the impression that I called him a twentieth-century Dr Johnson.

I

SEVENTY-SEVEN YEARS OLD: 1960

LORD Crawford, whose valuable term of office as Rector of St Andrews University had defeated vandalistic plans of the Scottish Office, was succeeded by Bob Boothby. When Bob was elected, a member of the Scottish Office said it was time that Rectorships at Scottish Universities were abolished as an anachronism.

In that February Bob wrote to tell me that he was Chairman of the group who were applying for the proposed I.T.V. station in North and East Scotland, and invited me to be a founder member. As usual he was blowing bubbles that seemed as permanent as crystal balls; in the end another group succeeded in obtaining what was to become Grampian T.V.

For years the B.B.C. had ruled against permitting Bob and myself appearing together in a TV programme. In that Spring they decided to take the risk of inviting him and me with Mark Bonham Carter to take part in a Brains' Trust. We were given a splendid dinner at Lime Grove. Gerald Beadle was the Head of TV and believed that a dinner in Lime Grove should be much better than a dinner in Broadcasting House. When we moved along to the studio Mark Bonham Carter had become completely de-wykhamised by that splendid dinner and was prepared to take the questions as opportunities for laughter like Bob and myself. It was an enjoyable three-quarters of an hour and even the camera-men were all laughing. However, the *éminences grises* of the B.B.C. were as little amused as Queen Victoria. I see now the expression of my cousin Leonard Miall as he observed on the way from the studio:

"Rather flippant?"

Bob was writing a day or two later:

"I'm not surprised that they won't let us on together again. Someone wrote from the North of Scotland: 'Sir Compton Mackenzie looked at you like a lioness inspecting her favourite cub.'"

A letter came that February from Nigel Nicolson which gave pleasure to Chrissie and Lily as well as to me:

"In the autumn of this year I am publishing an account of Lord Leverhulme's ventures in Lewis and Harris, and I had thought of dedicating the book to the memory of Malcolm MacSween. I enclose a draft of the dedication which I propose.

"I am sending it to you for two reasons. First, to obtain your permission to use your name in this way; and secondly, to ask you whether Miss MacSween would have any objections to my proposal. If she has not, could she supply the exact dates of her father's birth and death?

"I think that I am correct in saying that you sold the Shiants in 1936. There was another owner, a Colonel Macdonald, who held the Shiants for 12 months before I bought them, but I have thought it quite legitimate to leave out his name. I hope that you agree."

Calum MacSween had been the tenant first of Lord Leverhulme, then of myself and finally of Nigel Nicolson. Calum had been devoted to Nidgel as he always called him. I am thankful that he still owns those enchanted isles.

In that February I was shocked and grieved by the sudden death of Lady Mountbatten. I find the rough draft of the letter I wrote to Lord Mountbatten. I hope it communicates some of the distress I felt for the country's loss; the grief that India felt was movingly expressed by both Houses of Congress rising to stand in a devout silence:

"Feb. 22nd, 60.

"I hesitate to intrude on your sorrow with a letter, but I cannot resist adding one more heartfelt tribute to a great and courageous woman. It is not yet appreciated what you and she did for the Commonwealth in India and Pakistan. It will remain for me the outstanding achievement of statesmanship in my lifetime.

"Like so many many others I feel Lady Mountbatten's leaving this world as a personal loss. We cannot spare so brave and bright a spirit always diligent for humanity. We grieve with you."

In March my dearly loved niece Jean died. She was the only child of my brother Frank by his first marriage; the wife of Arthur Howard and the mother of Alan Howard. Lily had lived with her and Arthur for a time in their Emperor's Gate flat and Jean's death left a gap in the life of 31 Drummond Place which has never been filled. She was the victim of that merciless leukemia.

In that Spring I appeared on Professor Thomas Bodkin's *This is Your Life*. We had not met since 1924 when he was Curator of the Dublin Art Gallery. His daughter Mrs Vaughan wrote from Glasgow what gave me the best laugh I ever had from a letter:

Dear Sir Compton,

As Tom Bodkin's eldest daughter thank you very much. I briefed the script writer and hoped he might be able to persuade you to collaborate which in a way was Christian because you got me into an awful row when I was small and you visited 3 Wilton Terrace, Dublin and I was caught summoning my sisters to look through the sittingroom key-hole at a "madman in a skirt with a knife in his sock"—which must have been you. But then I loved you very much for writing 'Santa Claus in Summer'. Can't you get that reprinted so that my 5 children can enjoy it?

We knew your house when the Carrick Allens lived there and our first-born is an Edinburgh citizen who in her early days was sometimes dumped there while we went gadding. She's now 14 and doesn't like the idea that your sleep may be upset by the ghostly screams she left behind.

Mary Vaughan.

I was invited to speak in the Eights Week Debate at the Oxford Union. I look at the programme for Trinity Term 1960 and exactly ten years later read it with a faint depression over what could be a Trinity Term programme for 1970:

1st Week   April 28th.
      "That Parliament is failing the Nation"
Mr Michael Foot, Ex-President.
Viscount Hinchingbrooke, M.P.

2nd Week   May 5th.
    "That divorce by consent should be made legal in this
                  country"
Dr O. R. Macgregor, Author of 'Divorce in England'
Lord Birkett of Ulverston, Ex-President Cambridge Union.

3rd Week   May 12th.
    "That the Public Schools should be abolished"
Mrs Barbara Castle, M.P.
Sir Edward Boyle, Bart., M.P., Ex-President,
  Financial Secretary to the Treasury.

4th Week   May 19th.
    "That the South African Government's racial policies
  are incompatible with membership of the Commonwealth"
Mr Jeremy Thorpe, M.P., Ex-President.
Sir Oswald Mosley, Bart.

5th Week   EIGHTS WEEK   May 26th.
          To be recorded by B.B.C.
  "That this motion should be overwhelmingly defeated"
Mr Bernard Williams, Philosopher.

Mr Gwyn Thomas, of B.B.C., T.V. etc.
Mr Douglas Woodruff, Ex-President,
   Author of 'Plato's American Republic' etc.
Sir Compton Mackenzie, President of the Siamese
   Cat Club, Author of 'The Lunatic Republic' etc.

6th Week   June 2nd.
                Reserved for a topical debate.

7th Week   PRESIDENTIAL   June 9th.
   "That it is not one of the responsibilities of government to
        promote higher cultural standards"

8th Week   FAREWELL   June 16th.
         "Out, Out, brief candle!"

I have forgotten the details of that broadcast debate but I find a kindly letter from the Librarian to say that my speech had been much enjoyed.

In July to the grief of his friends and to the irreplaceable loss to his country and his party Aneurin Bevan died. As I record that loss ten years later I am more sharply aware than ever of that loss. Through the years of my friendship with Nye Bevan I watched him grow wiser every year and the wisdom he would have reached by now would have been of priceless service in this destructive world of today when mankind thinks that information is more important than education and that computers are a more reliable guide to the future than the oracles of ancient Greece, the prophets of the Old Testament and the saints of the Christian Church.

Faith's health was getting slowly worse all through the first half of this year. On the two last times I went to see her at the nursing home she did not recognise me. On July 9th she died. The Requiem Mass was said in the Carmelite Church, Kensington. The former church was destroyed in the blitz. The last time I had been in it was at Midnight Mass at Christmas 1900 when a soprano sang exquisitely the *Incarnatus* from one of Mozart's Masses, and when a few days later the Twentieth Century arrived in a shattering gale which felled one of the pillars of Stonehenge, an omen for this century of ours I have never forgotten.

This century was not yet six years old when Faith and I were married. She was five years older than myself and we could claim the secret of such a marriage was the ability of each to lead his or her life in mutual respect based on years of friendship. In some ways

Faith had been handicapped by her own versatility. If she had stuck to the piano she could have been another Myra Hess. I owed to her endless devoted hours of music while I toiled away at my earliest novels. She remained a marvellous accompanist. I recall Gerald Moore's once saying to me that she was the best accompanist he had known. However, apart from playing in trios with her sister Lucy, who was an accomplished violinist and member of a famous quartet, and her older brother Frank who was a good cellist, Faith gave up music to go on the stage. She was a good mimic but too self-conscious to be a good actress. Nevertheless, she had been on tour in the United States and played at the Avenue Theatre in London with Charles Hawtrey. I suppose Hawtrey himself had as it were escaped Eton to go on the stage and he had taken Faith into his company not because he thought she had the makings of a good actress but because he understood her anxiety to escape from, first, the atmosphere of an Eton House and then of the fashionable private school at Broadstairs owned by her father. As well as music and acting she was a first-rate caricaturist. Then she pottered about for a while with the beginnings of books. Then she took up sculpture and did some good work until she realised it was threatening her fingers with arthritis. Finally I set her down firmly to write a life of Queen Christina of Sweden which was published by Cassells and well received by the reviewers. However, her success came with her three volumes of reminiscences, *As Much as I Dare*, *More than I Should*, and *Always Afternoon*. They were published by Collins. When I started *The Gramophone*, Faith under the pseudonym F Sharp wrote many admirable reviews and also a remarkable quartet of essays on Rossini, Donizetti, Bellini and Verdi. I tried to persuade her to follow these up with Mascagni, Boito, Leoncavallo, and Puccini but she tired of opera composers and turned away from them to write a charming book about Napoleon on St Helena.

Faith was buried beside her mother in the graveyard of the little Catholic Church of Mortlake. In this graveyard is the strange dramatic tomb of the Burtons. It was appropriate that Faith, born beside the Thames at Eton, should rest beside the Thames.

I told in an earlier Octave of asking Eddy Sackville West if he intended to live at Knole after his father left it and how he replied, "Oh, no, it's much too suburban". He was true to that intention when he had become a Catholic and went to live in Ireland. Among the many letters of condolence I received I give here the letter Eddy wrote to me:

My dear Monty,

It was with real sorrow that I learnt of dear Faith's death and I hasten to send you my sympathy. I knew she had been ill for a long time, and I had not seen her since the war; but I recall many happy times with her in the rather distant past—her intelligence and humour and sympathy. There must be many who will miss her affectionate and charming personality.

I hope that you will not allow yourself to be too downcast and that your many friends may have opportunities of heartening you.

Ever

Yours affectionately,

Eddy

Another letter from my much loved parish priest at Northbay, Dominic MacKellaig, came from Roy Bridge:

My dear Monty,

I have just heard the news of Lady Mackenzie's death and wish to convey to you my very sincere condolences. May she rest in peace.

Faith was a very remarkable woman—so gifted and so witty. I remember well how very active and entertaining she was in the '30s. It was always most refreshing to listen to her conversation and her opinions. She was big in mind and soul.

These last few years were for her years of suffering which must have been very difficult. However, I understand that during the last few months she was not very conscious of things and that in itself was a relief.

I hope you are well yourself. I have not yet got the back right although it has improved a lot. My brother Father Angus has a parish at Easterhouse, Glasgow so I am spending the next fortnight with him, at the same time having treatment. I may go to the South with Father Neil after if I am fit enough to run around.

Will you please say a big thank you to Chrissie and Lily for being so kind to me while I was in Edinburgh. Having No 31 to go to made a big difference to me. All best wishes to you all.

Dominic

Dominic MacKellaig came to stay with us in Drummond Place while he was having treatment for his back. He went back to Roy Bridge and I was able to ring him up to congratulate him on being made a Canon. John MacQueen and Sydney McEwan had recently been made Canons of the Oban See.

"Canons to right of me, Canons to left of me," I said, "somebody has blundered."

I hear now his laugh. Two days later on Lily's birthday he died.

A letter from his younger brother Mgr. Neil MacKellaig, the Dean of the Isles, brings back happy times of which I have written in earlier Octaves. It was written after the funeral.

How very kind of you to write to me on this sad occasion—Father Dominic's death. We laid Dominic to rest in Cill-Chaorail yesterday. What an extraordinary situation for a graveyard! but what a gloriously lovely one! I don't know if you know it. From the crown of Dun an Aingeal, where he lies, there opens out one of the finest Highland vistas imaginable. The lovely Glen Spean, with its gorge and cascading river and straggling Scotch trees, lies far below. In the distance the Monadhliaths encase the picture. It is one of the finest inland views I know. Dominic loved such grandeur in life: he now lies where it is at its best. If ever you are in the district and have the time, the nerve and a driver willing to risk the mountain road I know you would feel well rewarded for the climb.

I often think back with pleasure on the very good time you gave Dominic and me in London, Oxford, Bath and Hampshire.

Alas, I must write of the death of another dear friend in that summer. 'Dick' Graves,[1] an older half-brother of Robert Graves, the poet and scholar of Mallorca, was in his third year at Magdalen when I was a fresher and always kindly. He was one of that remarkable family started by a Bishop of Limerick. He was at King's College, Cambridge, for a year to study Greek and Turkish for the Consular service of the Near East; which is what the ignoramuses of today call the Middle East. He had a successful career and his last job before retiring had been in Tangier. Dick Graves did not suffer fools gladly and at the Savile where he lived for some years he was known as *Graves Supérieur*.

My friendship with Dick Graves is expressed in some words his daughter Diana wrote:

"How very kind of you to write about Papa. He loved you so much and was always a new man when you came up to the club and he was able to have his long lovely talks with you. They always gave him such enormous pleasure.

"Papa was such a wonderful man as well as being a wonderful friend and father and I miss him dreadfully."

We were lucky to have at the Edinburgh Festival that year a German Ambassador who gave two splendid parties and was a man of exceptional charm. We had talked about Albrecht von Bernstorff. I wrote in Octave 7 of dining with Winston Churchill and

---

[1] The late R. M. Graves, C.B.E.

Bob Boothby in the Savoy Grill on that night in mid-November 1937 when Lord Halifax went to Berlin and Chamberlain's policy of appeasement 'escalated', as they say today.

From a generation ago I hear Churchill's voice:

"Well, Albrecht, I suppose your countrymen are making a fool of Lord Halifax tonight."

Albrecht von Bernstorff was one of those Germans stripped naked and slowly hanged before Hitler in April 1945, and the ceremony to which the Ambassador alludes in the following letter was the unveiling of a memorial to Albrecht von Bernstorff at the German Embassy in London:

"Back in London I would like to thank you for the inspiring hours I spent in your house. The guests included in your party could not have been nicer! I enjoyed every minute of it. May I pay special tribute to the wonderful food and those who were responsible for it! It was a real great evening for me which I will remember for a long time. I appreciated especially our conversation. It is such joy and privilege to listen to you with your excellent knowledge of the past and of great men you met.

"As soon as I know the date of the ceremony we will hold at the Embassy in order to commemorate Albrecht Bernstorff I will let you know. I hope very much that you will be able to come."

To my regret I was unable to attend the ceremony through one of my goes of pain, but I have included in Appendix E the typically thorough way in which the Germans managed such affairs. In my opinion Albrecht von Bernstorff was a heroic figure of Nazi Germany and the career of a German diplomat between the two wars seems worth recording.

It was in this September there came from the heart of Wales Bertrand Russell's appeal for civil disobedience to intensify the campaign for nuclear disarmament. He wrote to various people:

"The rapidity with which we are moving towards a nuclear calamity convinces me that events are moving too quickly for the present policy of our Campaign. It is my conviction that the effectiveness of our Campaign is becoming dependent upon its endorsing a programme of civil disobedience.

"I intend at the earliest possible moment to make a statement expressing the hope that the Campaign will become convinced of the necessity of such a programme.

"I should like to ask your support in carrying this into action. A group of one hundred persons called 'The Committee of 100'—for civil disobedience against nuclear warfare—is being formed and I should be grateful if you would join me on it. Could you favour me with an early reply?"

I joined the Committee of 100 but, alas, was unable to emulate that nonagenarian *hors concours* and sit down civilly disobedient in Trafalgar Square.

I am under the impression that the reason why I was unable to sit down in Trafalgar Square was the result of standing too long when the Archbishop of Edinburgh and St Andrews gave a reception for Cardinal Heard. I recall that after kissing his ring I said to the Cardinal, "The last time I saw your Eminence was on the towing path in shorts". As an undergraduate Cardinal Heard had been a valuable oar in the Balliol Eight.

In October came a grand invitation card which deserves printing, for I doubt if there will ever be another banquet in Edinburgh Castle for a King and Queen:

In honour of

Their Majesties the King and Queen of Nepal

HER MAJESTY'S GOVERNMENT

in the United Kingdom of Great Britain and Northern Ireland
request the honour of the company of

....

at Dinner, in the Upper Banqueting Hall, Edinburgh Castle
on Tuesday, 25th October, 1960 at 7.30 p.m. for 8 p.m.

The Right Honourable John S. Maclay, C.M.G., M.P.,
Secretary of State for Scotland, will receive the guests.

An answer is required to:

Evening Dress and Decorations.   The Private Secretary,
St Andrew's House,
Edinburgh.

When I had been in Katmandu thirteen years before the King of Nepal was almost a puppet in the hands of the ruling Maharaja family.

It was a good dinner with plenty of champagne. I was lucky enough to have the company of Lady Wheatley and Mrs Woodburn. The Lord Provost of Perth was sitting opposite and it raised my spirits about Scotland's future when I heard a Lord Provost talking so wisely.

Three days after that banquet I was on my way to Colchester for the Oyster Feast. In the train from Bishopsgate I found myself in the same compartment as 'Wully' Sempill,[1] 'Brab'[2] and the French Ambassador[3]. Brab was not willing to listen to any more talk about the future of flying from Wully and removed himself to another compartment. The French Ambassador was a distinguished old gentleman and I recall his reply when I said apologetically that I was finding as I grew older that I preferred sweet wines:

"Mais vous avez raison."

From that moment I have never apologised even in St Emilion itself for preferring Sauternes. I am still regarded with compassion by Scots when I reveal what they think is an unfortunate collapse of taste but I am not abashed. I recall that reassurance I was given by M. Chauvel.

At the lunch I found myself between the wives of two Privy Councillors neither of whom was evidently going to eat the half-dozen oysters in front of her.

"If you two ladies are not going to eat your oysters," I said, "do you mind if I eat them for you?"

And this I did.

The next course was turkey which I dislike and when one of the waiters who had noticed my eating the two ladies' oysters as well as my own asked me if I would like another dozen I gratefully accepted them instead of turkey. In Appendix F I have recorded the menu and the toasts of the Colchester Oyster Feast of October 28th, 1960.

"You've kept it very quiet, Ivor, that you are the Mayor of Colchester. Did you think it would worry *The Observer?*"

And I went on to tell the dramatic critic of *The Observer* (the last really good dramatic critic of any newspaper) that the Mayor of Colchester was Councillor Ivor Brown.

In the train home I had the luck to find myself alone in a compartment with Brab. When he reproached the lunch I bragged about the way I had managed to secure thirty oysters instead of the six everybody else got. I have a letter from Brab to remind me of that delightful railway journey:

"1st November. 1960.

"In that wonderful journey up to London, which I shall never forget, I promised to send you a copy of the book I wrote on my life

[1] The late Lord Sempill.   [2] The late Lord Brabazon of Tara.
[3] The late M. Jean Chauvel.

and this I am enclosing. Parts of it, like the curate's egg, may find favour in your eyes.

"Colchester Festival in my eyes (and in my stomach) was not a success. Six oysters, cold beef and some jelly, is not my idea of a feast, and 12.30 to 4 o'clock is a great part of the day wasted.

"However, curiously enough I look back on the day as enjoyable by virtue of your entertaining company on the way home.

Yours ever
Brab"

I still look back on that railway journey from Colchester with that youthful septuagenarian almost exactly a year younger than myself as the perfect way to pass a railway journey.

As I write in 1970 of my life ten years ago I find it a sad omen for the immediate future of Northern Ireland to read the following letter from the Secretary of the Campaign for the Release of Untried Prisoners in Belfast Jail. This letter was sent out perhaps appropriately on the eve of Guy Fawkes Day:

"For the past four years the Government of Northern Ireland has held up to 167 men in Belfast prison without charge or trial. It has claimed that these men are 'suspected' of connection with certain incidents (now long discontinued) on the border with the Republic. But no evidence whatsoever of any such connection has been produced publicly at any time.

"As a result of protests initiated by the Northern Ireland Council for Civil Liberties, considerable pressure has been exerted on the Belfast Government, and following resolutions from the British Trade Union conferences, the Parliamentary Labour Party raised the matter with the Home Secretary, who unfortunately took the view (disputed by leading Counsel) that he could not intervene.

"Even without the Home Secretary's intervention, however, the Northern Ireland Government then began to release prisoners in small groups, and as a result 100 have now been released and 68 remain in prison. No explanation has been offered for the choice of particular prisoners, but it is known that the Belfast Trades Council, the Transport and General Workers' Union, and the Northern Ireland Council for Civil Liberties made representations in certain cases.

"It is hoped to bring the Home Secretary to a fuller appreciation of what his responsibilities are in this matter. Meanwhile the men are still imprisoned and serious cases of hardship are known to exist.

"I feel that an effort should be made to appeal to Lord Brooke-borough, Northern Ireland Premier, direct, and therefore invite your signature to the following telegram which will be sent to him on the evening of a lobby of Parliament on November 9th:

"UNDERSIGNED URGE IMMEDIATE RELEASE EN BLOC OF REMAINING SIXTY EIGHT PRISONERS HELD WITHOUT CHARGE OR TRIAL IN BELFAST JAIL. WE CONSIDER FURTHER DETENTION UNFAIR AND CON-TRARY TO PUBLIC INTEREST AFTER 100 RELEASED ALREADY. CHRISTMAS IS APPROACHING. IN INTERESTS OF HUMANITY RESTORE THESE MEN TO THEIR FAMILIES."

The dark and foul mud of bigotry which was stirred up in the summer of 1969 by a Mr Paisley seems unlikely to sink back without more violence.

It should never be forgotten that one of the factors that con-tributed to the First World War was the belief of the Germans that Great Britain was on the verge of civil war. The weapons and munitions which were being imported from Germany to Northern Ireland without interference by the British Government and their use of the military to stop very much smaller importations of arms by the Home Rulers persuaded the Germans that, preoccupied with Ireland, we should not support France.

After what I consider the political crime which partitioned Ireland the Unionist Government behaved like barbarians by shutting up many Ulster Catholics in galleys. England, and London itself, had suffered once from the ferocity of Orange mobs but that was over two centuries ago and people in England could not understand the inspiration of such barbaric behaviour. But I must stop. I have not been able to regard Orangemen with equanimity since I was woken in the middle of the night by Orange tyranny in Londonderry eighty-five years ago.

When *Greece in My Life* came out, I sent a copy to Archbishop Makarios and was glad that what I had written of Cyprus and of himself had given pleasure. He wrote from Nicosia:

"It is an excellent book indeed. I have read it with much interest and many of its passages have left me in deep emotion. I hold in high esteem your adherence to noble ideals and I congratulate you for the love you feel for Greece. Cyprus owes a great debt to you for your moral support during her struggle to vindicate her right for freedom."

It had been a joy to me when at last it looked as if peace was restored to Cyprus. For that happier state of affairs the two people who could take most of the credit were the Archbishop and Sir Hugh Foot.[1] The former renounced his demand for *enosis* with Greece. I pray that a great man who has proved his wisdom and courage will be granted freedom from those plots of envious rivals to guide his beloved island.

We had a happy event with which to bring that year of much sadness to an end. That was the marriage of two very dear friends—Chalmers Davidson and Ursula Constable Maxwell.

I could not get down to Hampshire for the wedding but a letter from David Keir made me feel I had been present. I quote two or three lines:

"I went to Ursula's wedding with David Milne and Frank Newsam. Ursula looked radiant in a short and very attractive dress. Chalmers had a modest look of contentment with his lot."

I do not believe any other married couple had two Permanent Under-Secretaries at their wedding. I used to enjoy Frank Newsam's[2] company enormously.

[1] Lord Caradon.
[2] The late Sir Frank Newsam, G.C.B.

SEVENTY-EIGHT YEARS OLD: 1961

I HAD sent a copy of *Greece in My Life* to my old friend Bill Sells.[1] In it I had mentioned his invaluable help when I was prosecuted under the Official Secrets Act in January 1933. This was sent with my greetings for his eightieth birthday on January 19th, two days after my own and two years his junior. He wrote to me on February 2nd:

at Alverton Cottage,
Penzance.
2:2:61.

My dear Monty,

It was indeed a very great pleasure to receive your book with your more than kind inscription for both of which many many thanks. Also for your good wishes on my 80th—Ye Gods, how the years seem to flash by as one gets older— I am very lucky with only what I imagine to be a minimum of complaints due to the years and I hope your old troubles haven't been giving you too bad a time in these latter years.

Some eighteen months ago I passed through Edinburgh in someone else's car but we were on trek and had to keep to a timetable and I couldn't call in to see you if you were in residence as I wanted to do. If it happens again I shall hope for more time to find you with five minutes to spare for an old buffer. Incidentally it shook me rather to read your remarks in the book that Mrs S. and myself are the only people mentioned therein who are still about. I trust that she shares my good fortune in the way of health.

Your book must have entailed a vast amount of research and checking up— besides the exhausting job of racking your memory, astonishing though it is. I hope it has the success it deserves.

One of my greatest happinesses lies in having been able to retain (most undeservedly) the affection and regard of my two children. When Tony told me he was writing to get you to sign the book I thought it was rather cheek. But besides being a great admirer of your books—he has a lot of them including an unexpurgated copy of 'Greek Memories'—he still thinks I'm the cat's whiskers. I think the combination of the two sentiments gave him the temerity to attack you and it was good of you to play up so handsomely. Though slightly better educated than I was he's not the slightest bit intellectual and it will amuse you to hear that he has recently got off with, of all people, Edith

[1] The late Vice-Admiral W. F. Sells, C.M.G.

Sitwell—Osbert being one of his customers and very kind to him. When she was recouping in a nursing home recently he took her some flowers and to his astonishment she had him in for a chat. He reckons he's one of the very few people who have seen her in bed. I can't think how he gets away with it but it tickles me enormously and I believe she is giving him a copy of her next historical book.

I saw you a year or two ago being interviewed at home which you seemed to be enjoying very much—a bit of play-acting for you I expect—and I thought you looked very well indeed. Keep it up and take care of yourself and you'll find yourself 80 too before you can look around—you old rascal.

My love and thanks again for the book and your good wishes.

Yours

Bill

The way things were going in Cyprus made me happy. I had written to congratulate George Murray on a splendid leader he had written in the *Daily Mail* on 'Science and the Humanities'. In the course of his reply he wrote: "I thought of you when the Queen shook hands with Makarios the other day".

I had to write and congratulate Mrs Barbara Castle on the issue of that long, courageous fight of hers for justice to Cyprus and I was naturally touched when she was kind enough to write and tell me that my support throughout the 'beastly Cyprus business' had given her encouragement. I sometimes dream hopefully that one day Barbara Castle will be the first woman Prime Minister, but perhaps that is only another castle in Spain.

Two more old friends died early this year—Edward Longford[1] and Oliver Onions. Edward Longford's service to Eire was courageous and of immense value. I was sad to think I should not be seeing him in the autumn at the Wexford Festival.

It is sadly typical of the new *Annual Register* which started in 1958 that there is no obituary either of Lord Longford or Oliver Onions. The latter was one of the outstanding novelists of the twentieth century but the *Annual Register* was so pompously preoccupied with the imports and exports of small independent African states that space is now lacking for a record of the United Kingdom. On the bookshelves of my study as I write these words, I see the volumes of the *Annual Register* since it was founded by Edmund Burke over two centuries ago. They were bound for a long time in sober leather, later in sober cloth, until in 1958 they went into a gaudy binding

[1] The late Earl of Longford.

which did not compensate for their failure to register the social history of the United Kingdom and Eire instead of the imports and exports of African states. In fairness to the *Annual Register* of today I should say that its value for the social historian had been declining throughout the twentieth century.

I had dedicated *Cats' Company* to Elsa, the Queen of Cats, and I was much grieved to hear of the death of that noble lioness. Mrs Adamson wrote to me from Uganda:

"Dear Sir Compton,

I hope you will forgive this delayed thanks for your comforting letter, but things have been rather upset here and I could not write sooner.

"The cubs have reacted extremely wild since Elsa died. The first few days they kept hiding near the place where Elsa lived her last two days—obviously waiting for her—we heard them calling all the time. When I tried to spend a day near them they only bolted. Later they joined Father several times—but returned after 1–2 nights always hungry to camp about midnight, when everybody was asleep. I sleep in a lion-proof Land Rover next to the prepared kill to guard it against other predators who might frighten the cubs away. By these night duties I know exactly how often the cubs came for food—which was very irregularly.

"Since eight days they seemed to have joined a pride of wild lions as we found their spoors mixed and four nights ago they all came to camp—roared most impressively but did not touch the meat which was waiting for them. Since then we have no trace of the cubs. It is agony to be in this uncertainty but we have now no other means than spooring and we have lost their spoors.

"Of course it would be by far the best if the cubs could be adopted by wild lions who would teach them hunting—as they need at least another 6–8 months help. If they could only remain here in their home which has ideal conditions but we may have to remove them for polit. reasons and now—without Elsa's help such move means almost certainly disaster to the cubs. I so much hope they get taken over by these wild lions before ANYBODY can interfere with their future.

"Of course we will camp here as long as there is the slightest need for our help. In the meantime I am going more than ever ahead with raising funds for Game Preservation and have rewritten the appeal since Elsa died and hope that Collins has it already printed.

K

The wild animals are in such urgent need of help just to survive and especially with the political changes coming as well—every day is of importance to save them from getting exterminated for the benefit of developing schemes etc. I concentrated Elsa's appeal towards a scheme which moves animals from areas where they have to be shot because they clash with the interests of Man into areas where they are safe. These need at least six teams of staff and equipment—each costing 3–4000 pounds per annum—but these are the only means to save these animals. Elsa was herself twice a victim and got expelled from her HOME by THE AUTHORITIES—the last time on Xmas Eve. It was during the recess which my husband took to take Rudolf to find a new home for her that Elsa fell ill.

"She died of Babesia, a tick-borne parasite which destroys the red blood corpuscles. Elsa has been the first case recorded of lions. I cannot write what Elsa's death means to me but I am sure you understand. It was strangely timed.

"With many thanks again for your letter.

Yours sincerely,

Joy Adamson"

About a month after I received that moving letter our own beloved Bluebell, a Siamese blue-point, died of that infernal enteritis. She had been vaccinated against it as a kitten, and we did not know that as for human influenza this injection should be repeated at intervals.

Humphrey Hare had shown me a remarkable collection of cats' photographs by Richard Herzenberg. I made a selection of these and wrote a series of imaginary conversations by cats which I called *Catmint*. The book was published by Barrie and Rockliff in the autumn. It was dedicated to the memory of Bluebell.

In this Spring, Anthony Wedgwood Benn was fighting his battle to get out of the House of Lords and remain in the Commons. He asked me for a quotable message. I wrote:

"If the House of Lords can have Life Peers from the Commons, why can't the House of Commons have Life Members from the Lords, subject to the goodwill of the electorate?"

Wedgwood Benn's successful fight for a 'disappeerage' made it easier for other peers to escape.

In May the Royal Society of Literature announced the nearest approach in Great Britain to the French Academy. The British Academy has very little to do with literature.

"The Royal Society of Literature,
1, Hyde Park Gardens,
London. W.2.

"*To All Fellows*

The Royal Society of Literature has decided to create a new honour, with the title of Companion of Literature (C.Litt.) to be conferred upon a few writers who have given exceptional distinction to English Literature.

"This honour may be conferred upon men and women writers, whether or no they are already Fellows of the Society.

"The number of Companions of Literature will be limited to ten, who must be elected by a unanimous vote of Council. For the present, only five names have received this unanimous vote."

I should receive the C.Litt. with Dame Rebecca West, the late Dame Ivy Compton-Burnett and Sir John Betjeman in 1968.

In this year the Secretary of the Royal Scottish Academy wrote on April 27:

"I am happy to intimate to you that, at a General Assembly of the Royal Scottish Academy held on 26th instant, their unanimous Resolution of 18th idem to confer Honorary Membership on you as Professor of Literature was confirmed.

"I may add that the Professorship of Literature is purely nominal and involves the holder in no duties whatever, except to visit our Exhibitions and functions from time to time."

When the Royal Scottish Academy was founded under the patronage of George IV, honorary Professors of Anatomy, History and Literature were appointed to give advice and help to Academicians of the period. Painters no longer illustrate history or literature, so Sir Kenneth Clark and I are not overworked.

In the course of the early summer I had one of the worst goes of sciatic neuritis since coming to Edinburgh which, thanks to my devoted doctor Gilbert MacNaughtan and the air of that noble city, has brought me less pain than any of my previous homes. The maddening part of this attack was that it prevented me from accompanying John Campbell to Nova Scotia.

On February 14th Monsignor Somers, the President of St Francis Xavier University had written:

"This summer the Antigonish Highland Society, the oldest Highland Society in Canada, will celebrate the centenary of its founding. At the same time it will commemorate the One Hundred and Seventieth Anniversary of the arrival in Antigonish County of the first Highland settlers. These settlers were Catholics and were led by Father James Macdonald. They numbered four hundred and arrived in Pictou, Nova Scotia, in October 1791. They had been deprived of their lands in the Highlands and came from Arisaig, Knoydart, Morar, Eigg and Canna. The Pictou area in which they landed had been settled by Scottish Presbyterians and they continued into the next County, now Antigonish County. The new settlement they founded was known as St Margaret's of Arisaig. Nearby settlements were named by them Knoydart and Morar. They also named the highest hill in the vicinity Eigg Mountain.

"To mark the occasion, this University will have a special Convocation on Thursday, July 13th. The programme to mark the Centenary will begin on the previous Sunday and will end with the Highland Games on Friday and Saturday, July 14 and 15. These Games have been held annually in Antigonish for nearly one hundred years.

"On behalf of our University Council I am very pleased to ask you to honour the University by accepting the honorary degree of Doctor of Laws on this occasion. I trust that you will find it possible to accept. We shall be very happy if you could spend several weeks in Nova Scotia in July as the guest of this University.

"The Diocese of Antigonish is made up of the three Eastern Counties of the mainland and the Island of Cape Breton. They are joined by a causeway, which the late Premier, Angus L. Macdonald, named 'The Road to the Isles'. I believe you will find the scenery very fine and that it will remind you of the Highlands. In many communities are the descendants of the Highland settlers who have retained much of their Highland heritage.

"Dr John Lorne Campbell has visited Nova Scotia a number of times and plans to come here this summer. I am writing him today inviting him to attend the Highland celebrations. I trust that you will find it possible to accept our invitation and I can assure you of a very cordial welcome. You have many admirers in Nova Scotia. A reply by cable would be appreciated."

John Campbell who has what almost amounts to a passion for going backwards and forwards across the Atlantic in jet planes would have liked to fly. I was obstinate. The only way I would go to and return from Nova Scotia was by ship. So passages were booked to sail from Greenock to Quebec in the Canadian Pacific liner *Empress of Canada* on June 28th and return from Quebec to Greenock in the *Empress of Britain* on July 20th.

I was mortified and sadly disappointed when that infernal attack laid me out and prevented me from sailing in the *Empress of Canada*. I was able to record two speeches. One was in reply to the toast of our Celtic Heritage at the University Dinner on the evening of the conferring of the degrees. The other speech was for the opening of the Highland Games.

John Campbell wrote from Antigonish on July 11th:

"I hope you are feeling better now. Your photo and tape recording have arrived and have been welcomed. Everyone is very sorry you weren't able to come. Degree day is the day after tomorrow. The weather is peculiar—one day fine and warm, the next overcast with Newfoundland fog and cool."

The letter went on with what I felt was a faint reproach.

"Really the only way to get here is by jet to Halifax. At any rate it was a mistake to leave the ship at Quebec, I found; much better to have gone all the way to Montreal and got into one's sleeper there the evening of disembarkation. At Quebec it was necessary to carry hand luggage oneself across on the ferry to Levis and wait in the station until the train came in at 12.55 a.m.—though I had been told the sleeping carriage could be boarded there at 10 p.m. this turned out not to be correct."

And then at the end of a long and entertaining letter he wound up, "I shall take the jet from Halifax to Prestwick on the night of the 19th."

At the end of July I went down to London to attend the Annual Dinner of the Old Pauline Club. For years *Sinister Street* was regarded by some of the assistant masters and many Old Paulines as a misleading picture of the school. That I should one day be invited to propose the toast of the School to be replied to by the High Master would have seemed an utterly fantastic notion.

I was lucky enough to find myself sitting at dinner between Sir Colin Pearson,[1] the President of the O.P. Club, and the High Master.[2] I enjoyed so much the talk at dinner that I believe it had the same effect on my speech as champagne. Then of course I began to wonder if I had let my tongue wag too freely but I was relieved to hear from the Chairman of the Social Sub-Committee:

"May I, on behalf of my Sub-Committee, and indeed, on behalf of all Old Paulines present at the dinner last Thursday, express to you our most grateful thanks for proposing the toast of the School in

[1] Lord Justice Pearson.
[2] A. N. Gilkes.

such a delightful and reminiscent way. It was the making of the evening, and we are indeed very grateful to you for coming such a long way to undertake the task. It must be a long while since you sipped an aperitif under the bust of Dr Jowett in the Great Hall and had dinner in the School Dining Room. I hope you found the occasion enjoyable."

Indeed, I never enjoyed a dinner more.

I had been supposing that it was in the autumn of this year that I had a visit from an extremely perceptive young Indian who had been travelling round Great Britain. I find that in fact it was in October of 1959.

Sadhan Kumar Ghosh is now a professor of English Literature in Calcutta and his pupils are to be envied. I found in the course of our conversation that the impressions he had formed of various literary figures in England coincided exactly with my own. So naturally I was much impressed by his intelligence. He wrote an excellent little book, called *My English Journey*, about his visit to Great Britain, for which I tried hard to find an English publisher. Today, alas, publishers are at the mercy of printers and paper-makers whose ever-increasing charges may succeed in destroying genuine literature by the end of this century.

The critical articles by Sadhan Kumar Ghosh in Indian newspapers are models of the objective appreciation which the continuous effort to be 'with it' in London makes it hard to attain.

I shall not attempt to chronicle the functions I attended or the television and radio in which I took part. Indeed, I have forgotten most of them. However, I enjoy recalling a dinner at the Reform Club given to Ivor Brown on his seventieth birthday. There were twenty friends of Ivor Brown "to celebrate the occasion of his seventieth birthday and his contribution to the literary and theatrical life of our time". Norman Collins proposed the Toast to the guest of honour which was seconded by Colin Coote, Robert Morley and J. B. Priestley. It was an unhelpful move for British dramatic criticism when *The Observer* in an effort to be 'with it' replaced Ivor Brown by Kenneth Tynan.

Far away in Hong Kong another old friend of mine was being given a birthday dinner on November 1st to which I had sent Edmund Blunden my greetings. The University was lucky to have a true poet as their Professor of English Literature. He really would teach the students English Literature not Eng.Lit. Blunden sent his thanks in verse:

To the Company
Met for my Birthday, 1961.

When I was thirty-five, I think
I wrote a rhyme or two to say
"Time I went home". And fate said, stay,
Thirty years back, and *procul hinc.*

(Latin?), old Oxford's far from here.
How time has flown. Yet, "here I be,"
In village English, and "all we"
Assemble in this after year.

But what is time? some time we'll know,
And every day we count the clock
And wish its two hands would not mock,
Sometimes too swift, sometimes too slow.

It is not Prof. B. talking now,
But time's old traveller. Could he find
Expression for his heart and mind
As kind as you, sweet friends are kind . . .
All he can do is, bless, and bow.

Hong Kong 1 XI 1961   Edmund Blunden

At the end of the copy he sent to me the poet wrote in his enviable
handwriting:

> *Monty Mackenzie with*
> *E.B.'s many happy memories,*
> *renewed by his message to*
> *the Hong Kong front.*

Edmund Blunden and I had been members of the Book Society
Committee and always in agreement about choices and recom-
mendations.

I was elected Governor General of the Royal Stuart Society in
succession to the Duchess of Alba. I never had the privilege of meeting that great lady but I used to have enjoyable Jacobite talks with
her father when he was the Spanish Ambassador at St James's.
Legitimists recognised King Rupert of Bavaria as the representative
of the Stuarts, but for me the Duke of Alba was more representative.
He was directly descended from the Duke of Berwick and Alba, a
natural son of James II and VII by Arabella Churchill, a sister of

the Duke of Marlborough. Winston Churchill made the best case he could for his ancestor, but I feel that William of Orange was a disaster for Scotland, England and Ireland, and I regret that Marlborough, whose treachery to King James had ensured the success of that invasion financed by the gin-makers of Holland, was an Old Pauline.

A vivid memory of this autumn—I write 'autumn' and then begin to wonder whether it was not the beginning of 1962. I need hardly add that when I look in the *Annual Register* to see whether the prosecution of Penguin's for publishing *Lady Chatterley's Lover* as a paperback was in the autumn of 1961 or the beginning of 1962, I can find no reference to it.

On the evening after the jury had found in favour of the defendants I was dining at the Caprice restaurant in Arlington Street. Mario asked me to wait for two or three minutes in the little gentlemen's cloakroom until the table at which I was to dine was ready:

"And Mr Gardiner[1] is there. He's very happy this evening."

And indeed the future Lord Chancellor was sitting there looking radiantly happy. I apologise for the trite adverb but on this occasion it can be applied almost literally.

Gerald Gardiner had been of the greatest legal help to me at the time of *The Windsor Tapestry* over twenty years earlier, and he was a very serious young barrister in these days.

"You're looking on top of the world tonight. Congratulations, you certainly pulled off a marvellous verdict for Penguin's."

"The best I hoped for was the jury's disagreement, and I was very doubtful of securing even that."

I have paid a tribute in my book *On Moral Courage*, which was published in 1962, to the skill with which Mr Gerald Gardiner Q.C. persuaded the jury to argue the case among themselves for three hours and finally acquit Penguin's of pornographic behaviour. Nevertheless, I thought that some of the 35 witnesses for the defence talked pretentious humbug and canting balderdash in the witness-box.

I wrote in *On Moral Courage*:

"Two or three of the literary experts were boldly prepared to call *Lady Chatterley's Lover* one of Lawrence's greatest books, but most of them more discreetly refused to do this. When I was asked if I was prepared to testify I replied that I should be willing to say that Lawrence wrote the book under the impression that he was

[1] Lord Gardiner.

Pradelles

The Marty family

Ian Parsons and Norah Smallwood

writing a moral tract, but I should have to declare that as a piece of literature compared with Lawrence's best novels it was contemptible. That opinion I have held for thirty years and on re-reading the book that opinion has been confirmed. The literary judgments of one or two of those professors and lecturers in Eng. Lit. have filled me with a deep pessimism about the value of a University education today. If what we heard in court is to be accepted as the standard opinion of professors and lecturers, while we may still hope to see classical scholars in the future, there seems little prospect that the schools of English Literature will produce anything but young men and young women crammed with pre-digested courses, dehydrated information, tinned opinion, and desiccated taste."

And what I thought thirty years later I still think forty years later.

During that summer Margery Weiner sent me a clipping of an advertisement in *The Times* offering twenty acres of woodland, a barn and a three-roomed farmhouse for a sum in sterling. However, I decided to ask Chrissie what she thought of getting a place in France where we could feel sure of a good summer. Chrissie was captivated by the notion.

When I wrote to the young Frenchman who owned Pradelles, as it was called, I was worried to find that he wanted the money in French currency. He was working with the B.B.C. French department at Bush House. Finally, after a tiresome time I was able to be sure of the French money in October and I wrote accordingly to the owner. He wrote back to say that he would keep the property for me until I was able to pay the sum in francs to a local notary.

I had taken Chrissie and Mary Fay, my brother's daughter by his second marriage, to the Wexford Festival. We stayed at the Talbot Hotel and as always spent a week of unbroken enjoyment. When we got back Chrissie and Margery Weiner set out for France.

Jo Grimond had been elected Rector of Edinburgh University after James Robertson Justice finished his completely successful term of office. A Rector's job at a University was much more agreeable than it became a decade later with these small minorities of hairy fairies who try to make up with noise what they lack in brains and breeding. It was my good fortune to talk to the Freshers gathering in the Pollock Hall for three years in succession and I have not had better audiences anywhere.

I find a letter from the Convener of Lunchtime Addresses at the Union. I think that the bad manners in vogue as I write this last Octave are like the unpleasant acne which is the bane of so many young people. I feel sure that manners will be restored and that this letter will not seem a gush of eccentric politeness:

"I am writing to thank you for being kind enough to come along last Friday and give the Union such an entertaining address. Everyone has been very enthusiastic about it, and those of us who were present at the lunch and the conversation afterwards greatly enjoyed hearing your opinions.

"We should be delighted if you would care to come again, and bearing in mind what you said, next summer term would seem most suitable. We shall certainly give you an invitation at about that time.

"Once again, thank you very much for such a fine address on Friday."

Chrissie and Margery travelled by the night train from Paris to Cahors and after booking themselves in at the Ambassadeurs found a particularly good taxi-driver with whom they drove to Cazals. There they were told they were too late. Pradelles had been sold to an Englishman just the day before. They were depressed, and were much more depressed when they saw Pradelles and realised what they had lost. They looked at two or three other properties for sale in the neighbourhood but none of them was attractive enough to tempt Chrissie into considering it a holiday home. When they got back to their hotel they were told that there might be a 24-hour railway strike next day and were advised not to travel. So they drove around and looked at other properties always lamenting the loss of Pradelles.

When they came back to the Ambassadeurs they were told that the notary in Cazals had been ringing up to say he wished to speak urgently to the 'dames Anglaises' and would be ringing again later in the evening. It was after nine when the call was answered by Margery Weiner. It was to say that the Englishman who had bought Pradelles had decided on second thoughts that he did not want to complete the purchase after all. The notary was told that they were catching the eleven o'clock train for Paris in the morning but that they would drive out to Pradelles by half-past nine and take what the Englishman had rejected.

After a brief interview it was arranged that Chrissie would return early in November, and make the payment in francs. She was to be the owner of Pradelles.

At the beginning of November, Carol Costello drove Chrissie to Cazals to complete the purchase whereby Chrissie became the owner of Pradelles, to which Carol and she drove to sit on the large terrace in the benign sunshine of St Martin's summer.

Chrissie made friends with the Martys who lived in a two-roomed cottage about a quarter of a mile away on the other side of the road. Louis Marty was an elderly mason on the verge of retirement from active work but able to give valuable advice about any repairs immediately necessary. Mme Blandine Marty was a native of the Pas de Calais area of France and her first husband had been killed in the autumn of 1914 leaving her with a posthumous daughter. She had married Louis Marty when he was released as a prisoner of war and had by him another daughter, Louise Bonafous, who was separated from her husband and whose small son Max was living with her parents. She was working in a furniture factory some fifteen miles away. Madame Marty and Chrissie became friends at once. I was not to meet Madame Marty until next year but I recall being deeply impressed by a letter she wrote after Chrissie got back to Edinburgh. I felt that this was a woman of wisdom, humour and courage, and when I met her some months later I realised how right I had been.

I shall finish my seventy-ninth year by recording an experience of which I cannot find the date. The *Daily Express* rang me up one day to ask if there was anything I had not done which I should like to do. I was tempted to reply that I should like to visit the South Sea Islands, but as I gathered the *Daily Express* was preparing to fill this gap in my experience, I felt a voyage to the South Seas was rather too much to suggest. So I tried to think of something else and realised I had never glided and that gliding would be a novel experience I should enjoy. A day or two later the *Daily Express* notified me that arrangements had been made for me to go to Turnhouse to be taken up in a glider.

At this moment I ask myself in exasperation why I can remember in detail crossing the Irish Channel before I was two years old and why I cannot recall the details of that gliding hardly ten years ago.

What I can recall, however, as if it was yesterday is the exquisite sensation of being rocked in the cradle of the air, of the lowing and the bleating of cattle and sheep far below, of the sound of a church clock striking the hour. The only experience not available for myself at their age which I envy the young of today is gliding. In a jet plane I am always faintly anxious about its ability to stay aloft; in a glider I should feel much more surely air-borne.

O N January 23rd Chrissie and I were married in the Chapel of the Convent of All Souls on the other side of Drummond Place where I had always attended Midnight Mass at Christmas. The Convent is no longer there, its place being taken by a hostel for students who are much noisier neighbours for Willie and Fanny MacTaggart[1] than those sisters whose lives were devoted to the care of the poor and the sick.

As my one eye and I struggled to reach the end of this last Octave I find a long letter from Orlo Williams[2] which takes me back to the days of school, to Oxford, to Burford (it was he who found Lady Ham for Christopher Stone and me), to Gallipoli, for my reaching of which he was responsible, to Herm, to Eilean Aigas and indeed to myself in this eightieth year.

The first allusion is to a *Face to Face* I did with John Freeman. For many years now I have rarely got out of bed before mid-day, at first, because I had been writing all night, and later, because it had become a habit. The producer of this *Face to Face* had set his heart on my being in bed.

In the previous year, John Freeman had done a *Face to Face* with Gilbert Harding very shortly before he died, and he was unfairly criticised for provoking Gilbert's outburst of self-pity. The two interviews back to back are still obtainable on a record. Those *Faces to Faces* with John Freeman were supposed to reveal John Freeman as a formidable inquisitor. I found him as easy an interviewer as I ever had. I made only one stipulation:

"You are not to ask me about religion, John. What I can say in my own room to an Archbishop or a distinguished Jesuit I cannot say on television when I am seen and heard by simple Catholic folk."

John Freeman understood my point of view and religion was not discussed.

I recall saying when *Face to Face* was over.

"I think I chattered too much."

"That's what I wanted you to do."

And now here is that welcome letter from Orlo Williams who, alas, is no longer here to read what I am writing now:

[1] Sir William and Lady MacTaggart.
[2] The late Dr Orlo Williams, C.B., D.C.L.

"6 Weller Court,
66 Ladbroke Road, W.11.

"My dear Monty,

Tonight, after a solitary but pleasant supper here, listening in to a charming string quartet by Borodine, I feel impelled to write to you, for in the last week or so a large number of my friends have come singly and separately to tell me of kind allusions to myself which you made in your recent interview shown on the TV; and my sisters Gwen and Joan, whom you may remember and who are both in good active health (they live together at Bray), have had the same experience. My friends seem to have thought that it did me a great deal of credit, as no doubt it did, but sadly enough I did not see the broadcast, for I have no TV, nor did my sisters, nor did my daughter Rowena and her family, though they are keen addicts of TV. So, though I know in general, I do not know in detail what things you said, which is a pity. I wish I had been in on the event, but I just have no time to gaze into the screen; it would keep me from doing any reading at all.

"What I do know is that you received your interviewer in bed, and I liked the 'still' reproduced in the Sunday Times, for that showed you laughing gaily over a funny story, and your face then reminded me of days very long ago when I saw it laughing quite often—e.g., that night when we sat up at Imbros waiting and waiting for news from Suvla which never came, and you beguiled us all with admirable *contes drolatiques*. I hope, however, that your being in bed was nothing more than a matter of *mise en scene*, and had no significance as illustrating your state of health. And, by the way, let me wish you and Chrissie great happiness together! I regard your marriage as a most admirable move. I remember her first that time when I stayed with you at Eilean Aigas and particularly the day when, with you and her, I was taken over to Rum from Mallaig: and I remember her again the day when Eric Hazelton drove me over to visit you at your Berkshire Manor, the name of which escapes me.

"I hope you will not mind my typing this, which I do with my own hand, as I find it less fatiguing than penmanship at length, and if it should enter your head to send some kind of rejoinder, by all means dictate it to Chrissie, especially since I always found your pen-script rather difficult to read.

"I know you alluded to my part in getting you to Imbros in 1915, and it struck me how sad it was that, so far as I know, none of our friends of that time are still living. Guy Dawnay has gone, Cecil Aspinall has gone, George Lloyd has gone, the idle Keeling has gone, and I am sure Wardie has gone. The last of them whom I saw was Cecil Aspinall-Oglander, when he and his wife came to a talk that I gave on a poem of Leopardi's at the R. Society of Literature. That was certainly more than ten years ago, but I spoke with him on the telephone in the autumn of 1958 just as I was about to leave for my second visit to Rowena in Kenya. I promised to make a meeting with him when I got back, for he wanted to talk about Elizabeth Russell, having just read her daughter's biography of her, for he himself had known her quite well—a fact that was new to me. Elizabeth herself never mentioned his name to me. However, before I came back from my four months' stay in Kenya, Cecil had departed this life, and I see that his wife followed him very recently. He did not change much since Dardanelles days, his official history of which I always thought quite admirable. By the way, my own quite long and illegal war diary of that episode is now in the Imperial War Museum, and I daresay it contains quite a lot about you and all that followed your characteristic arrival (in that extraordinary uniform) on the scene. I told the Museum people that I did not want to keep it any more myself, and they could burn it if they thought it of little value. But I did not think they would when they read some bits of it. All they asked when they told me they would keep it was for a list of the proper names of those I mentioned by Christian name or nickname. This I gave them, but I told them I could not authorise them to do anything which amounted to publication till I was dead.

"I read that you are nearing the completion of an enormous autobiography which I hope I shall be there to read. I shall never do anything of that kind myself, in fact I have practically given up writing anything since my last book on the Clerks of the House of Commons, and I devote myself entirely to working at the piano, under the guidance of a well-known professor at the R.A.M., the wife of one of my Garrick friends who takes the trouble out of pure friendship. She says she is very pleased with the progress of her oldest pupil.

"I go to the Garrick a lot and have many friends there. One of the closest is that remarkable man Stanley Morison, for whom I have a strong affection and admiration. He once told me he knew you and that you had once eulogised to him my critical powers. I wonder when that was and how it came about; do tell me, if you can remember. Speaking of him leads my thoughts to the Times and the T.L.S., and thence to the cocktail party which Astor gave last

Wednesday to celebrate the 60th birthday of the T.L.S. The great thing was that Bruce Richmond, now 91 and very lame, was able to come up for the day by road from Islip, where he lives, and spend about an hour and a half sitting at the end of a large crowded room with countless people coming up to him. I was immensely glad to see him (and his wife) again in the flesh, and I thought he was in excellent spirits with quite unimpaired intellect.

"We *are* old, all the same. I wonder what you think of it and how you regard your life as it has turned out in comparison with the various daydreams of the future which you had when young. Mine rather surprises me, for I really failed to fulfil my early daydreams, but what I never would have dreamt of becoming, a proper D.C.L. (not hon.) of Oxford U. I did in fact become. It is the only achievement of which I feel proud, for it did not depend upon anybody's recommendation, only on the verdict of two unknown judges who had never seen me. But the things of which I feel glad and thankful are very numerous, and I am sure that is also true of you. And I am glad that the occasion of your TV interview brought our old acquaintance into your thoughts, and made me almost for a moment, a public notability.

With all greetings to Chrissie and yourself.

Yours ever,

Orlo"

Another letter from Orlo Williams shows that I was already working hard on Octave One of *My Life and Times*. Whatever trouble my one eye gave me on Octave One was nothing compared with its behaviour during Octave Ten:

"It was a great pleasure to get your letter of Jan. 30. Since then I have heard from my sisters that you made a very spirited and accomplished appearance in 'What's My Line', and I see that you were a guest at a Foyle lunch last week and have produced a book on Moral Courage. If you are writing 4 or 5 hours a day at your autobiography besides all this, you cannot have much sleep. I trust you thrive on this arduous regime, though I am sorry to hear of your trouble with your eyes. I am particularly interested to hear of your having taken a little French farmhouse in the Department of the Lot, with the aim of escaping summer callers. I am doubtful whether the aim will be achieved since nowadays all England seems determined to ooze over the Continent from July till late September. But I would like to know whereabouts your farmhouse is, not that I wish to be a caller or to divulge its whereabouts, but because I was touring last September in the Dordogne and the Lot with my friend Joan Saunders, Hilary's widow, in her car. What a lovely part of the world it is! We explored the middle reaches of the Dordogne well and all the side roads by the river. On our way westwards we had an entrancing drive from Figeac to Cahors along the winding road that follows the zigzags of the river Cele.

"I remember putting you up for the Savile very well and I am proud to have been sponsor for a Member with such a faithful record. Now that Bernard Wallis, whom I miss tremendously is no more, I am unlikely to go to my old club occasionally as I used to do with him."

On Moral Courage was published in February and had a kind reception from the reviewers and also from the reading public. Martin Secker reached eighty in April and it is a good omen for me that I should find a letter he wrote to me in that April for I feel that Providence will allow me to finish the last Octave in time to be published on my 88th birthday.

Martin Secker was still publishing books occasionally from 5 Royal Opera Arcade, but not long after this his failing eyesight led to his retirement:

"April 25 1962.

My dear Monty,

"I was so very pleased to have your letter on the occasion of my birthday. Becoming an octogenarian is really alarming, rather like receiving an O.M. but I suppose one gets used to it. I certainly intend to survive until 1966, so that I may enjoy my immortality in the third decade of your autobiography. I seem to remember that our first meeting, after some correspondence, was in 1910 on the occasion of the opening of the Temple Flower Show, which I suppose would be in June or July. I see you in a tall hat, morning coat and sponge-bag trousers, and wonder whether your recollection agrees.

"I greatly enjoyed your Collins' book, especially the two sections about D.H.L. What a lot of rubbish has been written and continues to be written about Lady C and the author's Message, whatever that was exactly. Now there is to be more in the forthcoming Encounter, following Sparrow's article.

"Thank you again for writing, dear Monty, and all best wishes now and always.

Ever yours affectionately,
Martin

P.S. In the Leavis-Snow controversy I am on the side of Dr Leavis all the time."

It was, of course, Secker who had published the first edition of *Lady Chatterley's Lover* with the four-letter words and botanical tricks of the gamekeeper excised.

I managed to finish Octave One early in May and we were happy to reach Pradelles by the end of the month.

It was in May that Willie MacTaggart who had received a knighthood in the New Year Honours had an exhibition of his paintings in the Stone Gallery of Newcastle-upon-Tyne. I was asked to write a few words about him in the catalogue and these words so express what I feel today about a lovable man that I cannot leave them out of this last Octave:

"It is my privilege to say a few words about Sir William MacTaggart, the President of the Royal Scottish Academy. I shall not venture to talk about his painting because I am not qualified to express any opinion about painting beyond the stale old ability to know what one likes; on those grounds I greatly admire what seems to me a rich and warm art. That warmth and richness is an expression of the man himself who is a very near and very dear neighbour of mine in Edinburgh. His friendship has been for me one of the great rewards of living in Edinburgh. I am a very hard worker myself and it is always a tonic to know that, on the other side of the Square where we both live, the brush is working just as hard as the pen.

"Sir William MacTaggart has done a great work for Scottish painting, but he is such a modest man that many people do not realise how much he has done. I love the man, and I have no doubt whatever that the City of Newcastle which has already recognised his great gifts, will accord him further recognition now. I myself only missed being a 'geordie' by a week nearly eighty years ago; I chose West Hartlepool instead. I have always enjoyed my visits to Newcastle and I wish I could be there this May to see how warmly Newcastle responds to my old friend Willie MacTaggart and his art."

The need to stick to my work had prevented me from going down to London for the opening of *A Thurber Carnival*. Helen Thurber had written a sweet letter to Chrissie and me on our marriage and in one sentence she brought back to me poignantly the memory of those two evenings with him in Edinburgh and the one evening in London. She wrote from the Savoy not from the Stafford Hotel where she and James had always stayed in London:

"I'm afraid a solitary trip to Edinburgh might bring it all back to me too strongly, but I would love to see you both here."

L

What a tragedy that James Thurber is not still with us to laugh at the moonstruck world of 1970.

The *Weekly Scotsman* which was a word from home to so many Scots all over the world is now, alas, defunct. The complimentary dinner given at the Westbury to the Scot of the Year nominated by the *Weekly Scotsman* is an occasion of the past. This year there were two Scots of the Year: Dame Flora Macleod of Macleod and myself. Dame Flora was unable to attend the dinner, but she was represented by her great-nephew Patrick Wolrige-Gordon, one of the Aberdeenshire M.P.s.

The menu was of course completely Scottish: Cock-a-leekie soup, haggis and the rest, but I wonder what one of the leaders of the Scottish National Party would have said to 'Moray Firth Scampi' instead of 'prawns'. The hysterical denunciation of the Common Market by the S.N.P. and 'jay-walking' with Douglas Jay is a sad betrayal of the auld alliance.

James MacPhee, the President of the Gaelic Society of London, was in the chair. Alastair Dunnett gave the toast to the two Scots of the Year as much to the point and as admirably concise as his speeches always are. After Wolrige-Gordon and I had replied there were speeches and whisky galore for the rest of the evening, and there were various gifts for the two Scots.

A young man in his early twenties came up to me to give me the kind regards of his mother and presented me with a double bottle of Cointreau. I wrote of that beautiful young woman, half Scottish, half Swedish, in Octave Eight. That was when the Saintsbury Club were the guests of the Club de Cent in Paris, and I had the privilege and pleasure of taking her in to the great dinner over which Sir Eric Phipps, our Ambassador, was presiding. That message from Madame Cointreau whom I had met only once a quarter of a century ago was for me the most enjoyable moment of a jovial evening.

Chrissie set out for Pradelles before me because I had tied myself up with several dates which had to be kept. Among them was a Foyle's Lunch to welcome Gerald Moore's book of reminiscences called *Am I Too Loud?* I was in the chair and a number of old musical guests came to support my tribute to the best accompanist that ever was, just as good, let me add, in conversation as on the piano.

There was a huge dinner at the Connaught Rooms given by the Pakistan Society, which Chrissie attended with me before she left for France. The top table alone had 52 sitting at it and there were

25 other tables. Chrissie was happy to find herself sitting next to Field Marshal Sir Claude Auchinleck. Our much loved Joe[1] made a capital speech proposing the guests which was replied to by the Aga Khan. The Pakistan Society was toasted by Duncan Sandys.

News came that the journey to Pradelles was successfully accomplished. Chrissie and one of her nieces were driven down through France in our new Citroen by Elizabeth Webb, an Australian friend, who was a successful broadcaster and was now writing a novel which would be published by Chatto's. She was the best woman driver by whom I have ever been driven.

I was preparing to write Octave Two during that summer and I thought I should like to revisit St Nazaire where I had spent the summer of 1894 with some other schoolboys. I used the experience in *Sinister Street*. I should have been wiser not to break my rule of never revisiting glimpses of the moon.

Antoine Girot of Air France, whom we had once had the pleasure of entertaining in Edinburgh, arranged for me to fly to La Baule and receive V.I.P. treatment at that little Breton airport, where Elizabeth Webb arrived with the Citroen. She and Belle, Chrissie's niece, had had quite an adventurous drive up from the Lot when they were caught by the tide somewhere and marooned till it ebbed.

There is no doubt that the people in that part of south-west France, where we had been lucky enough to find an ideal summer home, are temperamentally and even physically more like the people of north-west Scotland and the Hebrides than elsewhere in Britain. I found that Chrissie's French, the boredom of learning which she had endured at Kingussie Academy, had come back well enough for her to enjoy long talks with Madame Marty.

When I saw that enchanting wooded countryside I was back sixty years and four months ago when Harry Pirie Gordon and I were travelling from Toulouse to Paris after spending our Christmas vacation travelling in Spain and Morocco. We had been compelled to leave Barcelona without money or food because of the violent strike in January 1902. Hungry and tired as I was I had said to myself, "I must come back to this lovely countryside some day."

I soon realised that Pradelles would continually tempt us to make additions and alterations and improvements. I also realised that the Martys were both perfect *gardiens* of Pradelles when we were away but I also realised that they were both getting old. The problem was solved by the arrival of Louise Bonafous for a fortnight's holiday

[1] H.E. Lieut.-General Mohammed Yousuf.

from the furniture factory. I asked her what her wages were in the factory and made an offer of the same amount to be *gardienne* of Pradelles. That was eight years ago and when Lily and I reach Pradelles before a month is out (D.V.) Louise will be greeting us.

It was during the *vendange* Chrissie enjoyed herself most and she was as fast a plucker of grapes as any of the country folk round us. Hardly more than a year after that vintage Chrissie would have left us.

It must have been sometime in that summer which saw the publication of the Newest Testament. I must have made some disparaging remarks about it. An Emeritus Professor of Electrical Engineering at one of the new Universities wrote:

"I cannot agree that the new translation of the New Testament is valueless from a religious point of view. It has made its meaning clear to a lot of people who had no conception of what was intended by the Authorized Version.

"A number of scientists who have discovered the nature of the atom were my friends and their discoveries have increased my appreciation of the marvels of the Universe God created. The application of this new knowledge to produce the H bomb may be the work of the Devil."

I was impressed by the obvious sincerity of this letter, and although the N.E.B. will never be allowed on any bookshelf of mine and I regard it as one more nail in the coffin of English prose, I feel it is only fair to record another opinion.

October was crowded with engagements when we returned from Pradelles; I grow a little apprehensive about the possibility of my going gaga during the years left to me, when I find the menu of a dinner given in the 'refreshment department' of the House of Lords by the International Cultural Exchange World Organization, without remembering the occasion or the I.C.E. of which I was a Vice-President.

Here are the Toasts:

HER MAJESTY THE QUEEN
proposed by
The Rt. Hon. Lord Nathan, P.C., T.D., F.B.A.

TOAST FOR THE GUESTS
proposed by
Sir Compton Mackenzie, O.B.E., LL.D., F.R.S.L.
Vice-President, I.C.E.

Response by

The Members of the Diplomatic Missions representing:

Belgium: H.E. The Ambassador for Belgium,
                M. Jacques de Thier and Madame de Thier.

Brunei: The Agent for the Government of Brunei in the
                United Kingdom,
                Mr E. E. F. Pretty, C.M.G., D.S.N.B., and
                Mrs Pretty, P.O.A.S.

Ceylon: H.E. The High Commissioner for Ceylon,
                Mr R. Gunewardene.

Guatemala: H.E. Senor S. D. M. Miranda.

Jamaica: H.E. Mr A. Morais.

Nigeria: H.E. The High Commissioner of Nigeria,
                Mr Alhaji Abdulumaliki.

Switzerland: H.E. The Ambassador for Switzerland,
                Mr Armin Daeniker and Madame Daeniker.

United States: Vice-Consul and Third Secretaries to the United
                States Embassy,
                Mr O. S. Whittemore and Mrs D. McMeans.

United Arab   The Ambassdor for U.A.R.,
Republic: H.E. Mr Mohammed el Kouni.

I think I must have been so exhausted by giving the impression that I was listening interestedly to those ten responses that when the last one was given I forgot all about that evening of October 20th, 1962. I suspect that the U.S. Government was not enthusiastic about the future of the I.C.E. Indeed, the initials are not encouraging. I find it chilling that among all those Excellencies the U.S.A. should be represented by a Vice-Consul and Third Secretary to the United States Embassy.

I remember very much better the banquet of the Worshipful Company of Pipe Makers and Tobacco Blenders at the Mansion House on 16th October. Friends I had made when I was writing *Sublime Tobacco* were present. I sat next to Lady Hoare, the charming Lady Mayoress. I had an audience with whom I felt completely at one when I was replying to the toast of the guests given by Mr Frank Warwick, the Master.

The Senior Warden was W. A. Williamson-Barling whose firm of Pipe Makers in Camden Town was celebrating its 150th anniversary of its foundation. I was presented with a couple of perfect pipes as a well-known pipe-smoker. As I remember, J. B. Priestley was another who received this testimonial from the Pipe Makers.

The third Warden was Roy Bridgman-Evans, the representative by inheritance of Fribourg and Treyer, who will shortly be celebrating their 250th anniversary and are still in their original premises in the Haymarket, the most attractive shop in London.

Perhaps the fumes of peaceful pipes floated to Russia, for a day or two later a telegram came from Moscow:

"Moscow Literary Gazette arranges discussion on general disarmament which is ardently desired by Soviet people stop will you please write article expressing your opinion as to whether it is possible now or in the nearest future article 1000 words stop may we ask you to send your reply and your photo by airmail as soon as possible stop many thanks in advance.

Leontev Foreign Editor."

The Cuba crisis was now at its tensest moment. Kennedy had obviously been let down by American Intelligence and it was lucky for the world that Khrushchev was determined to avoid a Third War and able to damp down the militancy of the Soviet Armed Forces. I always feel that we do not yet appreciate Khrushchev's efforts to civilise the U.S.S.R.

I was much impressed by the Prime Minister's apparently complete lack of anxiety when he was the guest of honour at the inaugural dinner of the National Book Trade Provident Institution at Stationers' Hall. Sir Stanley Unwin, the President, introduced Mr Macmillan who then proposed the toast of the new Institution, which I seconded. I recall that the microphones still being used in Stationers' Hall were still the same as those of the B.B.C. at Savoy Hill forty years earlier. The Chairman of the Institution, Mr J. D. Newth of A. and C. Black replied.

I had never seen about 200 publishers or associates of publishers assembled. I feel sure that there must have been other authors present but I cannot recall one, and as I look back I seem to see myself like a Comma butterfly in a cloud of Meadow Browns.

There was a Foyle's Lunch at the Dorchester for Bob Boothby to herald the publication of his book *My Yesterday, Your Tomorrow*. It was a very pleasant surprise to find Somerset Maugham as one of the guests. One of the press photographers took a snap of us sitting with Lord Attlee and labelled it a 'A Trio of Octogenarians'. In fact Attlee and I would not be 80 until January when Willie Maugham would reach 89.

My next date with Bob that autumn would be one of his A.T.V. dinner parties which were having a success. He and his three guests ate well and when it came to coffee the conversation was recorded and immediately edited to appear at half-past ten on the same evening.

Bob Boothby's guests on this evening late in October were Hugh Gaitskell, William Clark and myself. Conversation at dinner was on different topics, but when the time came for the cameras to perform, Gaitskell asked to be given an opportunity to talk about the Common Market, our entry into which was being opposed by the Labour Party and by the Beaverbrook Press. It was hardly surprising that General de Gaulle did not view our entry with enthusiasm. Gaitskell himself was passionately against our entry and Bob Boothby boomed about the failure of the Labour Party in 1945 to support the Council of Strasburg of which he was a member, but he soon had to boom down and allow Hugh Gaitskell full control of the microphone while Clark and I sat silent. I was as much in favour of our entry into the Common Market in 1962 as I am today in 1970, because I feel that it is a step to achieving the European unity that is vital to the future of Europe if the civilisation of Europe is to endure. However, I am not equipped to argue about economics and therefore I kept quiet. I was talking about the autumnal beauty of the Lot when I shut up to avoid interrupting Gaitskell as he advanced against the Common Market like St George against the Dragon.

It was very soon after that dinner party that Hugh Gaitskell became seriously ill. His death in January 1963 was as severe a loss for the Labour party as that of Aneurin Bevan.

I have already in earlier Octaves tried to express how much I owe to 'Savilisation' since I became a member of the Savile in the autumn of 1912. In the autumn of 1962 I received this welcome letter from the Chairman of the Committee:

"I have the honour to inform you that the Committee of the Savile Club have unanimously elected you a Life Member of the Club, by virtue of Rule VI, which reads as follows:

"'The Committee shall have power by unanimous vote of the Members present at any of its meetings, to elect as a Life Member of the Club, without subscription, any Member with more than forty-five years continuous Membership, provided that the number of such Life Members shall not exceed ten at any one time'. "

The Savile had been such an influence on my life that I felt that this life membership was a happy omen for the publication of the First Octave of *My Life and Times* on my 80th birthday in January, and what seemed another happy omen was a television half-hour with Richard Dimbleby on New Year's Eve called *Goodbye Piccadilly*.

The producer had chosen the Café Royal as a suitable background, and thither Dimbleby and I repaired at an early hour on the previous Sunday morning to record the performance. Dimbleby was to do the commentary and I was to break in from time to time with reminiscences of two minutes, or one minute or one minute and a half, and these breaks had to be timed to the second. One second over and the break in had to be done again. I was sitting in a corner with the Café Royal mirrors on either side of me and the producer was so pleased with the reflection of my profile that he decided I should do all my chatter with those two confounded profiles. That meant I must not fidget or indeed move an inch to right or left. The Café Royal staff were hard at work preparing for Sunday lunch, so sometimes I would have to do my chatter again because of background noises, and perhaps again because I had been a second over.

Dimbleby as always was unperturbed and as always helpful to those on the screen with him. I used to get furious with people who objected to what they called his pompousness. No less pompous man ever lived and his loss to television and radio was immeasurable. He set a noble example of courage and I salute with reverence the memory of Richard Dimbleby.

By the time we had finished with *Goodbye Piccadilly* we felt we thoroughly deserved that excellent Sunday lunch.

As I was waiting in the Regent Street entrance for somebody who was calling for me in a taxi, a man with a much lined face for his age suddenly came over to me, offering a hand.

"At last!" he exclaimed.

This was W. H. Auden, the poet, whom I had never met. We had a brief talk and I much hope I shall meet him again some day for a much longer talk. That brief encounter was enough to reveal that he was a creative spirit, and that he had earned those lines on his countenance by devotion to his poetic ideals.

EIGHTY YEARS OLD: 1963

O N the eve of my eightieth birthday and the publication of Octave One of *My Life and Times* Chatto and Windus gave a large party at Carpenters' Hall. The Worshipful Company of Carpenters had just laid down a new floor and lady guests were asked not to wear what were called stiletto heels. Those high pointed heels were the most destructive fashion in which women ever indulged.

After the big gathering in Carpenters' Hall a party of intimate friends went on to the Garrick Club to enjoy a splendid dinner given by Ian Parsons (Ian Chatto of my dedication). Among the names signed on the menu I read *Christina Mackenzie*. Ten months later I should have lost her forever. Two other names on that menu can never be written again: *John Moore* and *David Keir*.

By ten o'clock next morning I really had reached eighty. Christina Foyle had gone to a great deal of trouble to make that lunch at the Dorchester a success. Here is Foyle's announcement:

FOYLE'S LITERARY LUNCHEONS

121 CHARING CROSS ROAD, LONDON. W.C.2.

Three-hundred and thirty-eighth Luncheon

on THURSDAY, 17th JANUARY, 1963

at 12.45 for 1 p.m.

A Luncheon in honour of

SIR COMPTON MACKENZIE

O.B.E., LL.D., F.R.S.L.

Guests of Honour:

H.E. THE HIGH COMMISSIONER OF PAKISTAN

LORD BOOTHBY, K.B.E., LL.D.

MR IVOR BROWN, C.B.E., F.R.S.L.

LADY VIOLET BONHAM CARTER, D.B.E.

DR DESMOND FLOWER, M.C.

MISS JACQUETTA HAWKES, O.B.E.

H.E. THE GREEK AMBASSADOR

THE RT. HON. THE EARL ATTLEE, K.G., P.C., O.M., C.H., F.R.S.

THE COUNTESS ATTLEE

MISS FAY COMPTON

MR HAMISH HAMILTON

SIR ALAN HERBERT

Lord Kinross
Mr John Moore, f.r.s.l.
Mr Ian Parsons
The Rt. Hon. Lord Reith,
    p.c., g.c.v.o., g.b.e., c.b., t.d.,
    d.c.l., ll.d.
Mrs Norah Smallwood
Dame Rebecca West, d.b.e.

Mr Cecil Day Lewis,
    c.b.e., f.r.s.l.
Mr J. B. Priestley, ll.d.,
    d.litt.
Mr Edmond Segrave
Mr William Kean Seymour
Mr Frank Swinnerton

Chairman:
Mr Rupert Hart-Davis

Chrissie sat next to one Excellency, our dear friend Mohammed Yousuf. I sat next to the other, the Greek Ambassador.

"You don't remember when we last met," said his Excellency.

"But have we met?" I asked in surprise.

"Yes, on Samos in April 1917 when I was a boy and my father was Governor. You taught us young people some new games at a party."

I was back in 1917 of which I wrote in *Aegean Memories*:

"Samos had immediately adhered to the Provisional Government and was now being administered by Constantine Melas. 'Coco' Melas was a fine figure of a man with a Vandyck beard and fierce mustachios. For many years before the Balkan War gave Samos to Greece it had been a semi-independent principality with a flag of its own and ruled by a Greek Prince appointed by the Sultan. Coco Melas was more like a Prince of Samos than a mere Governor. He and his wife held a kind of court which was attended by the prettiest girls on the island. We went to tea at Government House and played nursery games. I seem to see in a big drawing-room shaded by trees twenty lovely girls in white frocks and Coco Melas, with his back to a large marble mantel-piece, holding forth benignly on the ease of governorship.

" 'I thought when Mr Venizelos sent me here I was going to have a difficult job,' he told me, 'but it's the easiest thing in the world to be a governor. I've had no trouble of any kind.'

"And indeed there must have been some magic in the Samian air, because the first thing everybody told me was how splendidly somebody else was working and what a grand fellow somebody else was. After the bickering and squabbling and backbiting and grumbling all over the rest of the Aegean Samos was like a paradisal world before the Fall."

It was about a year after my birthday lunch that Michael Melas wrote to tell me that King Constantine of the Hellenes intended to make me a Knight Commander of the Phoenix. He was recalled to a high post in the Greek Ministry of Foreign Affairs and not long afterwards died depriving Hellas of a wise counsellor at a time when wisdom was much needed.

Rupert Hart-Davis was a splendid Chairman and made a speech which much moved me. I hope I managed to make the guests of honour and all the other friends realise how grateful I was to them for making me feel that I should be allowed to write Octave Ten of the life and times, the first Octave of which was published on that day.

I took the opportunity of paying a tribute to Lord Reith for his creation of the B.B.C. He wrote to ask me to let him have a copy of what I said for his diary. I had to write and say that I had spoken impromptu, but I was gratified to know that it must have pleased one of the really great men I have been lucky enough to know.

The wind-up of my 80th birthday celebrations was a party given by Joyce Weiner at Eyre Court on the evening of the Foyle's Lunch.

And now on June 13th, 1970 I come to the end of *My Life and Times* in this Octave. It has been a struggle because my one eye has been growing more and more tired all the time and the job of consulting old letters and papers a growing fatigue and irritation. Indeed, I might have found it impossible to continue without the help of my beloved Lily to whom I was married on March 4th, 1965. Her elder sister read my difficult handwriting with remarkable ease but it had become almost illegible even to myself by the time I set out on Octave Ten. Somehow she has been able to decipher what often I cannot decipher myself.

My emotion as I write these last words of a year by year record of a long life is one of gratitude. I have been happy and fortunate, *Homo Felix,* and I am still very happy and fortunate. As I lay down my pen on this June 13th, 1970, the feast day of my favourite Saint Anthony of Padua let my two last words be

DEO GRATIAS.

June 13th, 1970 in
31 Drummond Place, Edinburgh,
at 5.15 p.m.

APPENDIX A

REPORT OF TITLE

31 Drummond Place, Edinburgh.

The property consists of the maindoor and street flat, the two sunk flats, and three rooms below the sunk flats forming No. 31 Drummond Place, Edinburgh, and the ground or street flat and the lower of the two sunk flats forming part of the building which originally formed the dwelling house No. 32 Drummond Place, Edinburgh, and which has now been sub-divided into flats which have their entrance by No. 32.

There is also included in the sale the cellars in front of No. 31 Drummond Place and the back greens or back ground appertaining to both properties No. 31 and 32.

The feu-duties in respect of the two properties, which now form the self-contained flat, No. 31 Drummond Place, are £4.4.3 per annum for No. 31 and £3.4.6 for the parts of No. 32 now included in and forming part of No. 31 Drummond Place. These feu-duties amount in all to £7.8.9. The feu-duty of £3.4.6 is payable half-yearly (£1.12.3 at Whitsunday and £1.12.3 at Martinmas) and that of £4.4.3 is payable yearly at Whitsunday.

The Superiors are The Lord Provost, Magistrates and Council of the City of Edinburgh by whom the feu-duties are collected. The Titles also disclose a feu-duty of 1d per annum exigible in respect of the three rooms below the sunk flats forming part of No. 31 (this was at one time a separate dwelling house). This feu-duty is also payable to the Lord Provost, Magistrates and Council of the City of Edinburgh as Superiors, but we are informed by the Seller's Agents that it is not collected.

A garden assessment is levied on the property for upkeep of the common garden in the centre of the square but one-fourth only of the assessment is payable in respect of No. 32. The balance is payable by the proprietors of the basement, first flat, and top-flat properties. This assessment for the year to 28th February 1954 amounted to £2.5 – and has been apportioned as between seller and purchaser and paid. The assessed rental is £110 on which rates at 11/6 in the £ are payable each year.

The liabilities for the cost of repairs to the roof and for maintaining and upholding the common sewers and railings, are, as regards No.

31, apportioned at the rate of one eighth to each proprietor of the whole tenement. In the case of No. 32, the liability for maintenance is apportioned to one quarter on each proprietor. No proportion of these burdens applies in the case of the three rooms below the sunk flats which forms part of No. 31.

Although a right of access to the roof of No. 32 is given for the purpose of cleaning vents and other necessary purposes, by way of the entrance hall and stair of No. 32. no liability attaches for the maintenances of the entrance and stairway or the plat and stairs leading to the entrance or the railings bounding the stairs. There is however liability for maintenance at the rate of one quarter of the cost of any repairs to the railings bounding the street or ground flat which originally formed part of No. 32.

The two backgreens attached to No. 31 and 32 Drummond Place are included in the purchase and the cost of maintenance of these is your sole liability. The walls bounding the backgreens are, however, maintained mutually with the proprietors of the adjoining back-greens.

APPENDIX B

WAGERING CLUB

Bain Whyt is eleventh on list of original members on January 20th 1775, one of two Writers. Until 1816 the membership seems to have been drawn exclusively from worthy shopkeepers and merchants of Edinburgh with a steady number of Writers. It is significant that immediately after Waterloo the first Civil Servant should appear on the list in shape of Francis Gibson of the General Post Office. Any possibility of Wagering Club emulating Havana, Cosmos or Porch was averted in 1825 by making the Superintendent of Police, James Robison, a member. No Esquires appear until 1827 in the person of David Carnegie, a Captain. In 1831 the second Esquire appeared in the shape of William Fleming, Esq., Banker. Bank Agents of British Linen Company, Commercial Bank and Bank of Scotland have been elected but weren't allowed to be Esquires.

First record of bets in 1780. "It was suggested that it might be a matter of curious amusement as well as display the ideas from time to time entertained of passing events were the bets laid in future preserved or engrossed in a book, which, being accordingly resolved, the Clerk was requested to take and retain charge of them hereafter."

In that first year there were some military forecasts by armchair strategists, wrong as usual. Evidence of civic ambition in a bet that one of the Club would be a member of the Town Council before next year, and lastly memory of stirring times in a bet "that the trained bands of Edinburgh shall be equipped with firearms and military accoutrements" and of course they were not. They were probably given pikes. Then there's evidence of legal ambition in a bet that two Lords of Session shall not die. Nor did they. Six years later there was a bet that the Lord President would resign, but of course he didn't. There is a good rousing bet in 1781 that the privateer *Resolution* by the prizes it won would indemnify the subscribers. The privateer failed to do so.

Betting on marriages:

Miss Jean Campbell of Blythswood backed for matrimony in 1783 was still being backed in 1789. She faded after that from the scene either into matrimony or eternal spinsterhood, probably the latter. While Miss Campbell's chances were being backed one of the original members of the Club, James Brown betted in 1787 that I shall positively be married this year, signed James Brown. However, he lost this bet at the next meeting in 1788, and again in 1789 and 1790. This is strangely misplaced optimism because James Brown was a staymaker and if a staymaker doesn't know what chances he has of getting married I don't know what profession can.

Every year one or two of the young women of Edinburgh were being backed for matrimony before the year was out always I regret to say with a losing bet. In fact the only one who seems to have got married was Miss Dolly Dalrymple. The young women of Edinburgh must have thought the support of the Wagering Club was a hoodoo on their matrimonial chances, and the climax was reached with the sad record of Miss Allan, eldest of Hillside. She started being backed in 1821 and was backed every year until 1829 unsuccessfully. Whether in despair in 1830 Miss Allan, eldest of Hillside, drowned herself in the Water of Leith we do not know, but it is significant that when she vanishes from the records no more misses are backed. True Lady Margaret, a sister of the Duke of Buccleuch, was backed unsuccessfully in '30, '31 and '32, and then finally a last despairing bet was made in 1833 that one of the daughters of Viscount Melville would be married in a year, and alas not one of them was. After that Miss Burdett Coutts was backed for matrimony once, and finally Queen Victoria. That bet failed, but the following year at the dinner of 1841 she was backed to produce an infant before the end of the year and being Queen Victoria she succeeded. This might be described as doing the hole in one. Miss Boswell backed in 1792 to be married. Can this have been Euphemia, Boswell's second daughter, who left her family and proposed to live by writing operas. She would then have been eighteen.

In 1785 and '86 there is a sad story of thwarted hopes when William Muirhead who figures as No. 1 in the list of members was backed to get the warrant of brushmaker to the Prince of Wales, but alas, failed. In 1788 there is agreeable evidence of what a good dinner they all had the previous year in a bet that the Club last year dined in the room above that in which they are now assembled. This was in the Sommers Tavern. The bet was lost because they were dining in the same room. This seems an admirable example of what is called being slightly elevated by drink. In 1794 that Robespierre shall not be a leader of the National Convention in January '95. And now in 1798 we hear for the first time of Napoleon who would appear as a bet every year for 25 years. In 1798 Bunoparte shall not be allowed or known to be in existence on January 26th, 1799. This bet with the same spelling was repeated in the following year, but in 1800 the bet was that he would be allowed. In 1806 Bunoparte was changed to Bonaparte and do not let us laugh at the uncertain spelling when we remember that at least a couple of years round about 1920 *The Times* was speaking of an obscure figure called Hintler. In 1807 he was correctly spelt Buonaparte and in 1822 when he was backed to be alive by the beginning of the following year and died, the Secretary in making the record that he was so excited that he spelt him Buonaparte. By coincidence about this time the Club was dining in Oman's Tavern, Waterloo Place. In 1809, '10, '11, bets were being made that Great Britain and America would be at war within a year, but when they did go to war in 1812, both in 1813 and '14, bets were being made that they would be at peace within the year.

In January 1818 when we may hope that Bain Whyt was able to attend the dinner for he was to die in the December of that year, a bet was made that the Scottish Crown shall not be found in the investigation about to proceed respecting the ancient Regalia of Scotland. That bet, we are thankful to know, was lost.

In 1832 our world of today seems to begin with a bet that a railway shall be commenced between Edinburgh and Glasgow before the next meeting. The bet was lost, but the Reform Bill was passed that year. The railway between Edinburgh and Glasgow hung fire, and in 1835 a bet that a locomotive carriage would run for three months in continuation between Edinburgh and Glasgow was also lost.

In 1851 there is a poignant bet that intelligence of safety of Northern Expedition under Sir John Franklin be received, but that bet was lost.

In 1865 a bet was laid whether Great Britain would go to war with Prussia in defence of Denmark. How much of our modern difficulties can be traced to Great Britain's failure to support Denmark in the rape of Schleswig-Holstein.

Times of Dinner.

The first notice of a time in 78th meeting in January 1853 at the Café Royal, West Register Street, when dinner is at 5 o'clock. One may presume that until then it was at 4 or 4.30. In 1871 it was 5.30, in 1875 on 100th anniversary it was 6, in 1887 it was 6.30 and in 1937 it was the present hour of 7 o'clock. 1873 largest gathering yet.

M

Tom Hughes present. 1883, ten days after I was born, one of the bets was that the Botanical Garden would be open to the public on Sunday but the Sabbatarians were still able to resist that.

Nothing said about Bain Whyt in January 1819. That seems strange considering the passing of other members was so often treated with a solemn silence. Bain Whyt took chair in 1814.

APPENDIX C

West Bromwich.
16.5.54.

Sir,

I am reputed to be a busybody. May be, but a few days ago I read your article in the 'Spectator' on our West Bromwich Albion Football Club in which you say you had never found out why the boys are called the Throstles. I have had four homes in my lifetime: Yorkshire by parentage (Haworth); Derbyshire, Suffolk and for the last 28 years West Bromwich.

I am a retired teacher of History and Geography (aged 74) so you may perhaps gather that my interests are historical and topographical. I was intrigued by your admission, for 2 or 3 years ago Mr Stuart Hibbert was the principal speaker here at an anniversary meeting at our Throstles Discussion Group when I was President, and at a preceding lunch he propounded the very same thing and to my astonishment neither the Mayor nor ex-Mayor could enlighten him, showing how people generally take things for granted without going to the trouble to find out the reason.

The Grammar School Old Scholars are Old Throstles and we have several other groups of Throstles though only the Albion goes to the trouble of having an actual throstle in a cage which is brought into the stands for each match. Now for the reason.

Many years ago the town site at present was a wide heath with the Church, Manor House and farms and houses on the W.N. and E, Birmingham being 5 miles South. The main road from London to Holyhead passed through Birmingham and over the heath to Wolverhampton. On the heath donkeys and mules grazed and brayed. If a passenger was startled by a sudden bray and asked "What was that?" he or she was told, "Oh, it was only a West Bromwich throstle singing." Just a leg-pull really and I suppose everybody laughed. The name has stuck however.

Our boys are classically called the Throstles but as I suppose you know they are nicknamed the 'Baggies' because their knicks were generally wider than usual like those worn by Alec James some 26 years ago and they flapped in the wind like bags. Of course, the elite do not use that term but the general run of spectators do and the cry always is "Come on, the Baggies!"

My doctor tells me my ticker is tired so for 2 years I haven't dared to watch a match because of the danger of crushing but I can always follow the matches in our Birmingham Sports Argus and I am presuming to send you a copy of the Cup Final Edition which I don't think will have reached your northern home.

Perhaps by now you will think I really am a busybody. If so I can only plead that you asked for it in your article and hope you will forgive me.

I am, Sir,

Yours faithfully,

Jos. W. Proctor.

APPENDIX D

A Plaque unveiled in Chelsea.
From our London staff.

A distinguished company of artists, poets, painters, writers, actors and actresses, assembled in London on Saturday to salute the memory of Oscar Wilde on the centenary of his birth, and to assist in the civic recognition, modest but unmistakeable, of his work. Sir Compton Mackenzie unveiled a plaque erected by the London County Council on the wall of No. 34 Tite Street, in the Borough of Chelsea, to record the fact that Oscar Wilde, "Wit and Dramatist" had lived there. A Luncheon to celebrate the occasion was held later at the Savoy Hotel.

Nothing was more impressive in the commemoration than the size and nature of the crowd that gathered in Tite Street. The sky was dull and threatening. The setting has now no charm. No. 34 (which was No. 16 when Wilde lived in it) is a sombre, red-brick terraced house of four floors and a basement, and has been requisitioned by Chelsea to accommodate council tenants. One wall of the area has been whitewashed to give the basement's tenants a little more light. The house faces the Victoria Hospital for Children, which by its size makes the street look more cramped than it is.

Jostling among other spectators in Tite Street on Saturday were Mr T. S. Eliot, Mr Augustus John, Mr Sacheverell Sitwell, Dame Edith Evans (the Lady Bracknell of this generation), Miss Peggy Ashcroft, Mr Alec Waugh, Miss Isobel Jeans, Miss Margaret Rawlings, Mr Esme Percy, Mr Michael Redgrave, and Mr Michael MacLiammoir. The Irish Ambassador, Mr F. H. Boland was there with M. Boyer, representing the French Government, Mr Eugen Gurster, representing the Federal German Government, Dr H. W. Parke, Provost of Trinity College, Dublin, Mr C. G. Hardie, representing Magdalen College, Oxford, and Lady Cynthia Asquith representing the Pen Club. They all attended carefully while Mr Montgomery Hyde, Ulster Unionist Member for North Belfast and himself a writer, invited Sir Compton Mackenzie to unveil the plaque. They followed Sir Compton's speech closely and then welcomed the Mayor of Chelsea, Mr Guy Edmiston.

In a sense the Mayor was the most notable person present. The verdict of art has long been given to Wilde; civic recognition is the latest tribute to his work. The presence on Saturday of the Mayor and of Mr Fiske, chairman of the L.C.C.'s Town Planning Committee, deserves to be celebrated. The person who chiefly secured this result (apart from Wilde himself) was Mrs Irene Barton, honorary secretary of the Wilde Centenary Committee, who gave the L.C.C. no rest until it had approved the erection of a plaque. Oscar Wilde's son, Mr Vyvyan Holland, who had lived as a child in Tite Street, his grandson Mervyn, and Lord Cecil Douglas witnessed the proceedings.

It was the purpose of those who spoke on Saturday to make sure that the public should recognise the qualities of the man thus commemorated. Sir Max Beerbohm had first been invited to unveil the plaque but dared not exchange the warmth of Rapallo for the rigours of Chelsea. Instead he wrote this tribute which Sir Compton read out in Tite Street and repeated at the Savoy:

"I suppose there are now few survivors among the people who had the delight of hearing Oscar Wilde talk. Of these I am one. I have had the privilege of listening also to many other masters of table-talk—Meredith and Swinburne, Edmund Gosse and Henry James, Augustine Birrell and Arthur Balfour, Gilbert Chesterton and Desmond MacCarthy and Hilaire Belloc—all of them splendid in their own way. But assuredly Oscar in *his* own way was the greatest of them all—the most spontaneous and yet the most polished, the most soothing and yet the most surprising.

"That his talk was mostly a monologue was not his own fault. His manners were very good; he was careful to give his guests or his fellow-guests many a conversational opening, but seldom did anyone respond with more than a very few words. Nobody was willing to interrupt the music of so magnificent a virtuoso. To have heard him consoled me for not having heard Dr Johnson or Edmund Burke, Lord Brougham or Sydney Smith."

Another tribute which Sir Compton read twice was sent by Mr Laurence Housman:

"I am very glad that this memorial meeting is being held for so good a purpose. Oscar Wilde was incomparably the best talker I have ever met. But he was not only the best talker, he was also the most courteous and the most charming. His unhappy fate has done the world a signal service in defeating the blind obscurantists; it has made people think. For more people of intelligence think differently today because of him. And when he wrote his 'Ballad of Reading Gaol' he not only gave the world a beautiful poem but a much-needed lesson in good-will, pity, pardon, and understanding for the 'down and out'."

Sir Compton took up Mr Housman's theme. He recalled the public auction that had taken place "in the house behind me" when Oscar Wilde left the country. Sir Compton described the catalogue of that sale ending with a box of children's toys and a rabbit-hutch. He did not believe that the dreadful story of that auction would be repeated now. "I think today we are better, and I think we have had a great lesson", he said. Sir Compton returned to this subject when he spoke at the luncheon. He confessed that he had been a little worried recently by the methods of the Home Office and wondered whether they were quite right. But having raised this doubt, he reasserted his belief that there was more generosity and humanity today than existed in Wilde's time.

This was the essence of the public element in Saturday's ceremony, but a great deal more was said in praise of Wilde's artistry. Sir Compton described the excitement with which he, in his teens, had discovered the sophistications in Wilde's writing. "We felt that the world was coming to life again after the long, long sleep of the later Victorian age."

Mr Boland, the Irish Ambassador and a fellow-graduate of Trinity College, Dublin, with Wilde, gave a vivid sketch of Wilde's Irish origins and of his special debt to his mother, "known to us in Ireland as Speranza". M. Boyer, Cultural Counsellor at the French Embassy, read in French a tribute to Wilde from André Maurois, but based his own appreciation mainly on Wilde's association with Gide.

Herr Eugen Gurster, Cultural Secretary to the Federal German Consulate General, put a British audience to shame by saying that not a week passed without one of Wilde's plays being performed somewhere in Germany. "His plays", said Herr Gurster, "belong to the very foundation of the German Repertory theatre." And Mr Louis Wilkinson, the novelist, told of the generosity with which Wilde, then in Switzerland, had conducted a correspondence with him while a schoolboy at Radley.

Messages were read from Mr Walter de la Mare, and from Mr Allan Aynesworth, who was the original Algernon in "The Importance of Being Earnest". The Belgian French-speaking centre of the Pen Club also sent a message declaring that its admiration for Wilde was of the highest.

WILDE'S IRISHNESS
Emphasised in Dublin Tribute
From our Correspondent

Dublin. Sunday.

Oscar Wilde's "Irishness" was emphasised by Dr Lennox Robinson, the playwright, when he unveiled a commemorative plaque yesterday at No. 21 Westland Row, Dublin, where Wilde was born. "Had Wilde been alive 25 years ago when the Irish Academy of Letters was founded he would indubitably have been one of its foundation members," he said.

Mr Hilton Edwards, the actor, read a message from Mr Mac-Liammoir, who is acting in London, saying:

"Those of us in Ireland who admire Oscar Wilde's work and believe him to have been a man of great significance wish him to be remembered as a portion of that contribution which Ireland through a series of historical events has inevitably made to literature in the English language and to the tradition of the English theatre. We wish to remind our countrymen that Wilde was an Irishman, though like Shelley, like Baudelaire, like many artists, he was himself indifferent to nationality.

"We would have the passer-by remember that though it was England who gave him his fame and his infamy, it was Ireland who gave him those qualities that made him the most memorable tragicomedian of his age, it may be of any age. Those of us in Ireland who revere the best of his work, upon whom his personality has won an almost personal affection, are inclined to grudge the heaping of his gifts on the already rich lap of England."

FRENCH TRIBUTES.
Ceremony at Grave.

Paris. October 17.

Leading French literary figures yesterday paid tribute to the genius of Oscar Wilde, who was born in Dublin a hundred years ago and died in poverty here. Messages of homage, read during a ceremony at Père Lachaise, where Wilde is buried, came from three members of the Académie Française, André Maurois, Frenand Gregh, and Claude Farrere, and from Jean Cocteau. Sir Max Beerbohm also sent a letter of tribute from his home in Rapallo, in which he said:

"I have always been a great admirer of Wilde's essays. I consider myself most fortunate to have been able to listen to his unsurpassable and brilliant conversation."

An exhibition of Wilde's personal relics was opened at the hotel where he died, on November 30, 1900. The centenary was also marked by a public meeting at the Sorbonne and by a literary gathering at which extracts from "The Importance of Being Earnest" were read.

APPENDIX E

Biographical Data of Counsellor Albrecht Theodor
Andreas Count of Bernstorff

Born on the 6th of March, 1890, in Berlin.

Nationality: Prussian.

Religion: Protestant.

Father: Count Andreas von Bernstorff. Wirklicher Geheimer
(imperial title, bestowed on Under-Secretaries etc., and carrying the form of address "Excellency"). Oberregierungsrat (chief
privy councillor), Kammerherr (chamberlain), Fideikommis-
besitzer (owner of an entailed landed estate): Stintenburg near
Lassahn, Duchy of Lauenburg, Schleswig-Holstein. Member of
the Reichstag 1894–1904.

Mother: Augusta, *née* von Hottinger.

School: Private tuition up to the age of 16.

February 1909:   School-leaving certificate at the Kgl. Kaiserin
Augusta-Gymnasium (grammar school), Berlin.

University Education:

1909–   SS. University Berlin for studies in jurisprudence
and political science.

1909–1911   At the proposal of the Emperor William II.
(October 1909– Cecil Rhodes Scholar at Oxford, Trinity
July 1911)   College. Studied political economy and political
science: Diploma in Political Economy and
Political Science.

Military Service:

Oct. 1911–   Enlisted in the Dragoon-Guards as a volunteer,
April 1912:   then transferred as unfit for military service to
the Landsturm mit der Waffe (armed veteran
reserve). Conclusion of Law studies at Kiel;
passed the first civil service examination in
Law at the Provincial Court of Appeal at Kiel,
June 19th, 1914.

July 1st, 1914:   Junior barrister at the Provincial Court of
Appeal at Kiel, transferred for further training
to the Law Court (petty-sessional and county
court) at Plon.

Since 1907: Owner of the Stintenburg Estate in the district of the Duchy of Lauenburg. Deputy of the district-council.

"Diplomatic" Relations:

Grandson of Count Albrecht von Bernstorff, who from 1854–73 at first represented Prussia and subsequently the German Reich as Ambassador at the Court of St James.

Nephew of Count Johann Heinrich von Bernstorff, 1902–1906 Counsellor at the London Embassy, Imperial German Ambassador in Washington (1908–1917), died at Geneva in 1939.

Nephew of Count Percy von Bernstorff, President of the administrative district of Kassel.

(Albrecht von Bernstorff gave the names of these relations as references in his application for admission to the diplomatic service.)

Dec. 29th, 1914: Summoned by the Reich Chancellor, von Bethmann-Hollweg, to a post unpaid at the Imperial German Embassy in Vienna (Ambassador von Tschirschky and Bogendorff) for a period of six months. Attaché as from January 1st, 1915.

June 2nd, 1915: At the proposal of the Reich Chancellor, given leave of absence until December 14th by the Minister of Justice for service at the Vienna Embassy. (Such leaves of absence were granted regularly on the application of the Foreign Office, until von Bernstorff left the legal service in 1920.)

March 10th, 1916: Awarded the Austrian War-cross of the 3rd class for distinguished civil service.

Sept. 29th, 1917: Summoned to service at the Foreign Office by Reich Chancellor, Dr Michaelis. Transferred to Department 111 for further training (legal department).

Nov. 10th, 1917: Transferred to Department 11 (commercial policy).

Oct. 11th, 1918:	Assigned to Wirklicher Legationsrat, Dr. Riezler.
Nov. 8th, 1918:	Appointed Legationssekretar, "with the prospect of permanent establishment".
Sept. 10th, 1919:	Took oath of allegiance to the Republic.
Jan. 12th, 1920:	Since December 28th assigned to Department A.H., L. 8a (German–Austria, Czechoslovakia), for informative employment.
April 10th, 1920:	Delegated by a decree to assist and deputise for the Geheimer Legationsrat, Dr Mudra, with the "Representative of the Foreign Office with the Reich Commissar for the Occupied Territories of the Rhineland" at Coblenz. Took up post April 15th.
May 11th, 1920:	After recall of Dr Mudra, von Bernstorff remained as "Representative for the Foreign Office with the Reich Commissar for the Occupied Territories of the Rhineland".
Feb. 9th, 1921:	Appointed established Legationssekretar, effective as from March 1st, 1921.
Nov. 18th, 1921:	Released from his duties at Coblenz, as "Representative for the Foreign Office with the Reich Commissar for the Occupied Territories of the Rhineland".
Dec., 1921– Dec., 1922:	Unpaid leave at his own request for training in the banking business. (Private banking business of Messrs Delbruck-Schickler & Co., Berlin.)
Dec. 14th, 1922:	Transferred by decree to the German Embassy in London as Legationssekretar.
Jan. 20th, 1923:	Took up duties at the London Embassy.
Aug. 31st, 1923:	Appointed representative of the Embassy Counsellor, von Kamphovener.
Sept. 22nd, 1923:	Given the official title of Embassy Counsellor.
April 26th, 1924:	Appointed Embassy Counsellor of the 11 Class.
Aug. 7th–Oct. 15th, 1930:	Chargé d'Affaires, representing the Ambassador and the Embassy Counsellor.
Feb. 12th, 1931:	Appointed Embassy Counsellor at the London Embassy.

June 24th, 1933:   Called to the Foreign Office in Berlin by the Reich Foreign Minister, von Neurath.

July 3rd, 1933:   Reported to the Reich Foreign Minister, von Neurath. On the instructions of von Neurath, von Bernstorff returned to London from July 20th–August 8th.

Nov. 25th, 1933:   Placed in provisional retirement with the legal retaining-pay by deed of Reich President von Hindenburg.

March 23rd, 1937:   Placed in permanent retirement in accordance with paragraph 6 of the Law for the Re-establishment of Professional Officialdom of April 7th–June 23rd, 1933.

Dec. 14th, 1944:   Expulsion from his status of a retired official by order of Hitler "on account of his participation in the events connected with the attempted murder of the Führer on July 20th, 1944". A copy of this notification addressed to von Bernstorff by the Reich Minister and Chief of the Reich Chancellery, Dr Lammers, was sent under date of December 18th, 1944, through the Reich Minister of the Interior to the Ober-reichsanwalt (chief Reich counsel) Lautzat at the People's Court.

APPENDIX F

GRACE BEFORE THE FEAST
by the Mayor's Chaplain
(THE REV. D. R. TASSELL, M.A.)

MENU

Colchester 'Pyefleet' Native Oysters
Brown bread and Butter, Lemons
Roast Norfolk Turkey, York Ham, Ox Tongue, Game Pie
Roast Beef
Salad of Potatoes, French Salad, Russian Salad
Rolls and Butter

Peach Flan and Cream, Charlotte Russe, Assorted Meringues
Fruit Cocktail Jellies, Gateaux

Cheese and Celery, Biscuits

Dessert

Coffee

TOAST LIST

1. THE QUEEN

2. THE HOUSES OF PARLIAMENT
   Proposed by: F. H. LAWTON, ESQ., Q.C.
   To Respond: THE RT. HON. GEORGE BROWN, M.P.

3. THE LAW AND DEMOCRACY
   Proposed by: KENNETH HORNE, ESQ.
   To Respond: ANTHONY GREENWOOD, ESQ., M.P.

4. THE ART OF LIVING
   Proposed by: THE RT. HON. THE LORD BRABAZON OF TARA,
   P.C., G.B.E., M.C.
   To Respond: SIR COMPTON MACKENZIE, O.B.E., HON.LL.D.,
   F.R.S.L.

5. OUR DISTINGUISHED VISITORS
   Proposed by: V. G. HINES, ESQ.
   To Respond: THE RT. HON. DOUGLAS JAY, M.P.

GOD SAVE THE QUEEN

APPENDIX G

The Antigonish Highland Society
1861–1961

The history of the Highland Society dates to August 22, 1861 when the first meeting was held "to preserve the martial spirit, language, dress, music, games and antiquities of the Caledonian, for relieving distressed Highlanders at a distance from their native homes, and for promoting the improvements and general welfare of our native country". This is a direct quotation from the original minutes of the organisation which was first known as the Highland Society of Sydney. Sydney then comprised Antigonish and Guysborough Counties. The tartan officially adopted by the Society was the tartan of the 42nd Regiment.

The first President of the Society was Dr William Alexander MacDonald who emigrated from the Isle of Skye and was descended from the Lords of the Isles. Affectionately he was known as 'Old Doctor Bill'.

At a meeting held on December 13, 1862 at Duncan Chisholm's Store the following resolution was adopted:

"Resolved that in the opinion of this meeting it would conduce materially to carry out the objects of this Society that prizes be offered for competition in Highland Games and that such prizes be offered during the course of the ensuing year to be followed in the evening by a Ball at the expense of such as would participate in the amusement of the evening."

The first Games were held on October 18, 1863 on Apple Tree Island, the beautiful ground of W. C. Hierlihy, Esq. The Casket of the day carried the following account: "A more fitting and beautiful place for these exercises could not have been selected, and the day was all that the most ardent admirer of the sports could have desired. The Society formed in procession, headed by their banners and pipers and the games were opened by numbers of ladies and gentlemen taking part in the Scottish reels on the green sward around the musicians' platform."

The Games began officially and the Casket again reports: "Such was the display of muscular energy and athletic ability that we are inclined to think that our Games will favourably compare with those of any other Society."

The Games were carried on thereafter for several years. It was customary for members to meet and march in procession to the grounds where the Games were held and begin the proceedings with a Highland Reel, danced in real Scottish style by members of the Society.

On September 14, 1871, the Games were held on Cathedral Hill, the net proceeds of these Games being donated to Bishop MacKinnon for the building of the new Cathedral.

The Games lapsed for several years but were resumed in 1919. Since that time they have been regarded as the Premier Braemar of Canada. The Society has done much to encourage and promote Highland Dancing and Piping, as well as track and field competition. Each year over 100 young pupils are trained in a dancing school directed by the Society. The re-organisation of the Highland Pipe Band has also been a recent achievement with the co-operation of Arras Branch of the Royal Canadian Legion. The Highland Society Track and Field team competes favourably at all major events of this kind in the Maritime provinces.

The Society has also been prominent in charitable and patriotic works as befitting the ideals of their early members and they were largely instrumental in the erection of the handsome memorial to the veterans of the First Great War in Antigonish. On several occasions the proceeds of the Games were devoted to charitable projects such as St Martha's Hospital, the Queen's Canadian Fund, and the Red Cross.

The Games have grown and expanded to such an extent that at least two days were required to run off all the events four years ago. The Province of Nova Scotia regards this annual event as one of its leading tourist attractions. Accordingly, the Highland Society is proud of its presentation and expresses the wish that everyone— visitors and residents alike—will join in the spirit of the occasion and enjoy themselves to the full.

INDEX

OCTAVES NINE AND TEN

N